What They **Don't Teach** in Prenatal Class

What They **Don't Teach** in Prenatal Class

The Key to Raising Trouble-Free Kids & Teens

Anne Andrew, PhD

Clear Purpose Publishing

Copyright © 2019 by Anne Andrew, PhD. All rights reserved.
No part of this book may be reproduced, stored in a retrieval system, or transmitted by any means, electronic, mechanical, photocopy, recording, or otherwise, without written permission from the author.

Client names have been changed throughout the text.

Author photo by Jennifer Shoshana Hulman
Cover and interior design by Constellation Book Services

ISBN: 978-1-7752583-1-5

Publisher's Cataloging-In-Publication Data
(Prepared by The Donohue Group, Inc.)

Names: Andrew, Anne, 1958- author.

Title: What they don't teach in prenatal class : the key to raising trouble-free kids & teens / Anne Andrew, PhD.

Description: [Vancouver, British Columbia] : Clear Purpose Publishing, [2019] | Includes bibliographical references.

Identifiers: ISBN 9781775258315 | ISBN 9781775258322 (ebook)
Subjects: LCSH: Self-esteem in children. | Self-actualization (Psychology) | Interpersonal communication. | Parenting. | Children--Conduct of life.
Classification: LCC BF723.S3 .A54 2019 (print) | LCC BF723.S3 (ebook) | DDC 155.4/182--dc23

Printed in the United States of America

Dedication

To my beloved, miraculous daughter who taught me more than I ever expected to know about Love—I'm forever grateful!

Contents

Foreword by Diederik Wolsak, RPC, MPCP   ix
Introduction   1

PART ONE. The Key to Happiness: Inherent Worth

Chapter One: What I Wish I'd Learned in Prenatal Class   9

Chapter Two: Is There a Problem with Self-Esteem?   18

Chapter Three: How to Help Children to Recognize and Own Their Inherent Worth   30

PART TWO. Unconditional Love: A Parent's Guide

Chapter Four: Do We Really Know How to Love Unconditionally?   53

Chapter Five: How to Disable Your Buttons: Removing Your Barriers to Love   78

Chapter Six: Happy Parents, Happy Kids   93

PART THREE. Parenting Priorities: Kindness *Versus* Grades

Chapter Seven: Parenting with Purpose   119

Chapter Eight: Strategies for Raising Kind Kids   130

Chapter Nine: Parenting with Love and Not with Fear   140

Chapter Ten: Your Role as a Parent   154

Appendix A: Resources and Recommended Reading   163
Appendix B: Are you Parenting out of Love or Fear Quiz   170
Appendix D: Raising Bully-Proof Children   175
Appendix E: The Radiance of the Lights   186
Appendix F: References and Citations   195

Acknowledgments   203

Foreword

It is two in the morning and you have no idea where your daughter is, who she is spending time with, or how to reach her.

The school contacts you with the distressing news that your son has not been to school in days and they would like to know if he is alright.

Your mother wonders how it is possible that her savings account is $200 short; how could that have happened?

Your son does not have many responsibilities but the one he has, doing the dishes, has become a nightly battle.

You've noticed that your daughter seems to eat heaping servings of salad every day, and she is still losing weight. You don't really understand what is wrong here: salad is healthy, isn't it?

These and so many other frightening experiences are all too common in far too many families. How can we, parents, raise our children so we are not seemingly suddenly faced with challenges such as the above?

The book in your hands by Dr. Anne Andrew provides you with invaluable tools, profound insights, and compassionate solutions to raising children who will not make you question your sanity or even your fitness to be a parent.

Above all it is a masterful practical guide to the Joy of Parenting.

Dr. Andrew's writing is all the more poignant because it is not some clever academic piece of theoretical suggestions to ease the stress of parenting. No, Anne Andrew has written a manual which draws directly from her own heroic and victorious battle with depression and her transformation of some crippling core beliefs. But more to the point it tells the story of two people, parents, coming to terms with what *they* needed to heal to become real parents. Real parents teach by demonstration. Real parents are transparent and not afraid of what they'll encounter when they begin their own journey to removing all barriers to love.

You see, our kids watch us, all day. Our kids are keenly tuned in to our insecurities and deeply treasured core beliefs. Our kids at a very deep level take on responsibility for all *our* failings and make these their own. There is no exception to this. Beliefs run in the family. This has little to do with "genes" and everything to do with our children being egocentric, meaning that their entire world revolves around them. If their parents are happy, they must be OK. If there is financial strain in the household, for example, the children may develop a belief that they are a burden or they may decide at age one that life is hard.

Anne Andrew and her husband encountered challenges with their daughter that few of us will ever have to face. They very quickly accepted the simple fact that *if* they wanted a different experience with their daughter they had to do their own work and be totally focused on their own process. The fascinating part of Anne's story was that initially their daughter wanted to have absolutely nothing to do with "therapy" ("I've seen one hundred therapists; I doubt you'll be any different"); however, not long after both Anne and her husband set off on a journey of discovery and healing, their child voluntarily came to see me: "I have no idea what you are doing with my parents, but they are changing."

Once the child knows that he or she is not a cause but an effect, healing can begin to take place. Anne Andrew has called on decades of experience as an educator as well as on her remarkable talent to challenge her disciplined mind in a direction which affected the entire family—and now, through this fabulous book, potentially untold others. Anne has a deep understanding of the psyche of a young person, a fierce commitment to her own continued healing, and a refreshing honesty about the challenges she met in the process.

Read this book, reread this book, and practice the steps Anne Andrew teaches here and you will find that child-rearing becomes in so many ways a perfect vehicle for self-healing.

If you are looking for simple, direct teachings to help you find a new level of delight in being a parent, this book provides all the practical information you'll ever need.

Diederik Wolsak, RPC, MPCP
Program Director
Choose Again Attitudinal Healing Centers
Costa Rica and Vancouver, BC
Author of *Choose Again: Six Steps to Freedom*

Introduction

"One thing I had learned from watching chimpanzees with their infants is that having a child should be fun."
−Jane Goodall

Are you anxious about how one or more of your children are turning out?

Is parenting more of a struggle than you anticipated?

Are you confused by the number of parenting styles and opinions?

Do you feel judged whenever you are out with your children no matter what they are doing?

Do you feel responsible for your child's happiness or lack of it?

If you answered yes to any of these questions, then this book is for you.

My experience as a worried parent of a once troubled teenager (now a well-functioning adult), and my wish to help other parents avoid the sleepless nights, debilitating fear, helplessness, and despair, led me to write this book. Our family's ordeal lasted more than six years, and during that time we learned strategies that not only helped us survive but actually allowed us to thrive. As we learned to cope with our family situation in the best way possible, we turned our lives around and emerged stronger, a closer family unit, with greater clarity, increased happiness, and a sense of joy that had not been present.

At the same time, I was working as a school principal and became aware of the mental health crisis that was starting to take hold in younger and younger students.

The statistics are disturbing; for example, 77 percent of children report having been bullied at school, and 80 percent of ten-year-old girls wish they were thinner. It's likely that one or more of your children will face some kind of difficulty, whether it's an eating disorder, bullying, drug addiction, depression, or other mental health issue, and it is almost impossible to predict whose child that might be. You can't always see it coming—we certainly didn't!

Wearing my educator's hat, I took what I was learning from our family's therapist, analyzed it, saw the evidence, and concluded that there is an absolute and fundamental concept that underpins healthy human life. This concept, if taught when children are very young and reinforced as they grow up, will result in resilient kids who are not only mentally healthy, but bully-proof, addiction-resistant, and kind. It is this concept that forms the basis for this book and underlies the other strategies that were so impactful for every member of my family. That's right! Just one fundamental concept!

My work environment provided a place to test the techniques that I was learning along the way. These included:

1. Introducing a guided meditation and mindfulness practice—long before it was as commonplace in schools as it now is. Teachers reported how much calmer the children were, and that they were able to teach more effectively as a result. Students loved it and it increased their sense of spirituality enormously.

- ❖ If you don't already have a meditation or mindfulness practice I'll be encouraging you to adopt one and show you how you can incorporate it into family life.

2. Recognizing that behavior problems in students were the natural outcome of the negative beliefs they already had, and that any disruptive behavior was a cry for love. My remedy was to extend love and to problem-solve with the disruptive child—it worked like a charm. I saw behavior problems as opportunities for growth—for both the student and for me!

- ❖ I'll encourage you to see your child's behavior problems as opportunities for growth for both of you.

3. Reframing any conflict with a parent, teacher, or student as an opportunity for healing one of my own negative beliefs. I had the tools to take the emotion out of it so that I could deal with a neutral problem to be solved jointly. It always worked.

❖ I'll show you how to do this. When you work on problem-solving without emotional involvement you'll discover how much more creative the solutions will be for both you and your child.

4. Instituting a school-wide gratitude practice and learning the profound effect that this had on the students, particularly in enhancing their sense of wonder, and in not taking things for granted.

❖ I'll give you lots of suggestions for ways to practice gratitude as a family—it is possibly the single most effective method of heading off teen problems!

It was, seemingly, my daughter's troubles that brought me to change my way of thinking about parenting, teaching, and life in general, and it is my professional background that has allowed me to translate what I learned into concepts and strategies for parents and teachers to use. I retired from my teaching position to spend my time developing a program to help parents raise trouble-free children. This book has grown out of those workshops and is organized into three parts:
Part One, "The Key to Happiness: Inherent Worth," will introduce the fundamental concept of Inherent Worth that's at the core of this parenting technique. This is the guiding concept that I wish I had known before my children were born and which I hope will become a primary concept for parents and teachers to reinforce throughout a child's life. I tell my daughter's story briefly in Chapter One, but beyond

that it is irrelevant to the rest of the book. Chapter Two looks at the difference between self-esteem and Inherent Worth, then Chapter Three lists nine strategies for helping children to own their Inherent Worth.

Part Two, "Unconditional Love: A Parent's Guide," explains the importance of loving our children unconditionally. It will explain why it is so difficult for us to accept and own our Inherent Worth, then explain how this can be done and become part of your "way of being." Most of us don't know how to love our children unconditionally because we have barriers to love in the form of negative beliefs. Chapter Four will explain how negative beliefs get started, how they drive behavior, and how they block love. Chapter Five will show you how they can be transformed using the Choose Again Six-Step Process. Chapter Six will give you examples of ways in which using the six-step process can be applied in your day-to-day parenting and gives examples of problems that can be tackled with it.

Part Three, "Parenting Priorities: Kindness *Versus* Grades," will look at parenting priorities. Chapter Seven encourages an examination of the purpose of our lives and suggests that kindness is more important than grades (though they are not mutually exclusive). Strategies for raising kind kids are given in Chapter Eight. Chapter Nine teaches how to parent out of love—not out of fear, which is the essence of this book. My list of strategies for effective parenting is given in Chapter Ten.

The result for you, the reader will be:

- ❖ a new perspective on the role of a parent, which will decrease the amount of stress that you may be currently experiencing.
- ❖ the tools you need to deactivate your buttons, diffuse conflicts, and thus increase the amount of peace in the home.
- ❖ fearless communication among the members of your family.
- ❖ strengthened family relationships.
- ❖ an opportunity to significantly improve your own happiness and stress levels and become much more in control of your life experiences.
- ❖ an understanding of how to avoid the emotional (and financial) costs of dealing with troubled teens.

There are helpful practical suggestions for improving the mental health of every family member. I know that if you are able to implement some of the techniques taught in the following pages, your experience as a parent will be a joyful one and you'll greatly reduce the chances of your children becoming statistics. My hope is that you'll be able to learn from my experience and use my strategies to change your parenting approach if needed. By making some changes, you will find that you and your family will be far happier than you ever imagined...

PART ONE

The Key to Happiness:
Inherent Worth

Chapter One

What I Wish I'd Learned in Prenatal Class

"The day you were born was the day God declared that the world could not exist without you."

–Nachman of Bratslav

A few hours after my daughter was born, she was given a bath by a nurse in the post-natal ward. My daughter's obvious delight at being in the water brought an image to my mind. There she was, a beautiful athlete, standing on an Olympic podium receiving her first medal—for swimming. In hindsight, that should have been a big red flag—we were heading for trouble!

The Early Days

Our daughter's first years seemed happy enough and we had no reason for any concern. As parents, we were busy with work and outside commitments, but we didn't think this was out of the ordinary. In hindsight, we didn't have enough fun on a regular basis with our kids, though we did take them on outings to the aquarium, science world, waterparks, and all the usual childhood attractions. I was a frequent driver on school field trips and ran the "Safe Arrival" program to make sure that all the children were accounted for at school in the morning, so I was visibly involved in my children's education. Both our kids had music lessons, sports activities, and religious education (at the supplementary school where I was principal), so they were quite heavily programmed, although we didn't think so at the time.

The Downward Spiral

At the age of twelve, my daughter started to lose weight. My husband was on the Weight Watchers diet at the time. We were eating healthy meals and didn't notice that she was restricting her eating beyond what was good for her. A routine visit to the doctor's office resulted in an aberrant point on her growth chart that showed her weight less than it should be for her height. Following a visit to a specialist at British Columbia Children's Hospital, she was given the diagnoses of anorexia and bulimia. We were shocked. How had this happened? It would be a few more years before we had the answer.

She received years of treatment mostly as an outpatient, but also as an inpatient for a few weeks, which helped her to recover from anorexia, but the bulimia persisted. During one of our weekly visits, I remember reading the posters on the walls at the eating disorder clinic analyzing data from a study of the link between eating disorders and smoking—in fact, many of the patients did smoke. I noted the study and hoped that my daughter would not be one of those that turned to smoking.

Unfortunately, smoking did become one of the ways that she felt she could control her weight—this despite her having been an outspoken anti-smoking campaigner at her high school. Drinking and other self-harming behavior soon followed. The downward spiral accelerated at an alarming rate. She started cutting classes, attending raves in distant towns, and visiting her drug-addicted boyfriend. In just a few months, she went from a well-functioning, high-achieving student to high school dropout.

Life quickly became unbearable. Our child, who was so adored, behaved in ways that were inexcusable and unfathomable. We didn't know which way to turn nor where to find help. It was as if we were groping helplessly in the dark for an increasingly elusive way out. At the same time, our son, who had breezed through elementary school and was given an award as the top all-around student in his eighth grade year, became school president at the high school they both attended. His sister's behavior was a source of embarrassment to him in that capacity. He went away to university in part to escape the increasingly fraught atmosphere at home. It became apparent to us later that his striving for external "success" was a result of the same parenting style that led his sister in the opposite direction, and years later he did his own inner work to improve his happiness and his relationships (at home and at work).

The Way Back Up

Eventually, by word of mouth, we came across an incredible therapist (Diederik Wolsak, RPC MPCP), and with his help, things slowly started to turn around. When I first took my daughter to see him, I told him that she needed help. He smiled and suggested that I could only work on myself, and that it would help her if I did. She would be able to help herself when she was ready to do so. He suggested that I come for a few sessions first. I was skeptical—I didn't see how that could possibly help—but we were desperate, and so I went. It took my husband a little longer, but he eventually came too.

That decision—to work on myself—was the best choice of my life and transformational in so many ways. It only took a couple of sessions before I was actually feeling euphoric. I had released some closely held beliefs about myself that were preventing me from experiencing joy in my life. I didn't even know I could feel so happy! I was able to turn my life around from being stuck in a never-ending cycle of depression and anti-depressants to one of joy and gratitude. I went from being angry most of the time without understanding why, to being calm and at peace frequently, able to handle difficult situations with ease. I went from being a workaholic with a single focus to having a balanced life and enjoying exercise, hobbies, and various crafts. I'd never allowed myself to pursue these interests without feeling guilty for what I perceived as wasting valuable time.

My daughter's mood lightened because I was no longer being dragged down by her, so a layer of her guilt was lifted. Our co-dependent relationship was untangled and I was able to see her as a wholly worthy human being despite her behavior. The love that I had for her returned in a huge wave. The changes that she saw in me, and in her father, prompted her to work on herself, and she was able to turn her life around in a remarkable way. It wasn't a quick fix—we all had to do our work diligently—but it worked.

One Fundamental Concept

I was able to discern that there was one concept at the core of this therapeutic program that was fundamental to the changes that were taking place. This one concept was responsible for my husband's recovery from the stress of his career, my recovery from chronic depression, and the recovery of countless others of Diederik's clients from depression and substance abuse (Warren Helfrich, 2014). It saved our daughter's life. This concept works as an antidote to the negative beliefs that drive the self-loathing that underpins so many mental health issues. It is the concept applied in Step Six of the Choose Again Six-Step Process (Diederik Wolsak, 2018)—Diederik's main therapeutic tool—which I present in this book as a useful tool for parents.

So, what is this concept? Expressed simply, it is that each of us has Inherent Worth just by being. We need do nothing to earn it and it can never be changed. This concept is both obvious and radical. It is obvious, because we all come into the world equally naked and leave it the same way. It is radical, because as a society we use a ranking system where we are all stacked up against each other and try to get as far up the ladder as we can. We are trained and encouraged to pursue our worth "out there"—in our education, our career, our relationships, and virtually every aspect of our lives. We are persuaded by the media that our worth depends on the latest iPhone or the swankiest sports car. This has led to the idea that our worth depends on external factors, whereas it is actually an inside job—it's inherent.

What Does It Mean That Our Worth is Inherent?

Well, if our worth is inherent, it stands to reason that our worth is *not* established by:

- our wealth,
- our career,
- how thin we are,
- how good we are at math,
- the clothes we wear,
- how many "likes" we have on Facebook or Instagram, nor followers on Twitter.

It is easy to see the truth of this when a baby is born. No one comes into the world any other way. As we grow up we become aware of our appearance. People react to us and judge us, we gain an education, acquire toys—first teddy bears, later coffee makers. We gain status, more toys—a house and a car if we are lucky. But all these distractions can obscure our true self from us. We are like layers of an onion. The innermost layer is who we truly are—pure, innocent, whole, worthy. The layers represent our external status—our relationships, careers, possessions, dwelling places, talents, hobbies, and beliefs. The external factors serve to obscure our inner self, our true worth, from us. When we are able to see that the outer layers are just noise (even the good stuff, such as the university degrees), then we can connect with the truth of who we are and be aware that our innermost self is still there—lovely, pure, and totally worthy. This pure self cannot be affected by anything we do or don't do. We need to teach children that not only do they have this innermost layer—Inherent Worth—but everyone else does too. It would be difficult for a child who understands this to be a bully (or a victim, for that matter!).

The Pursuit of Happiness

There is a gruesome saying that I hear often from parents: "I'm only as happy as my least happy child." I'm going to challenge that line. Happiness is an inside job—it is not our child's job to make us happy. Similarly, we can't make our children happy. Having said that, this book is about laying the foundations so that our children will best be able to find happiness within themselves. My happiness comes from knowing my Inherent Worth.

It is a very simple premise that by owning your Inherent Worth (IW) you can be happy, and that this is the single most important concept to convey to your children so that they can avoid the pitfalls as they grow up—simple, but not easy. A closer look at the entire meaning of this concept is the subject of the rest of this book.

What I Wish I'd Learned in Prenatal Class

I opened with the image of my daughter's first bath. In hindsight, this was an indication that I needed her to complete me in some way—to provide me with the sense of worth that I lacked. The subconscious message I gave her was, "You have to bring me happiness and pride"—that, of course, paved the way for her to do the exact opposite. If I had understood at that time that my own worth was inherent, the thought of her Olympic medal would never have crossed my mind. It would have been perfectly clear to me that my worth is not established by having a daughter who is an Olympic athlete, and she would have been free to discover her own passion. What I learned the hard way is that my only job as a parent is to love her, appreciate her, and discover who she is. Her job was to be a child and to follow her heart. As easy as that sounds, this book and the workshops I lead came out of my quest to learn how to do that.

Recovery from mental health issues such as substance abuse and depression can happen by recognizing that we have Inherent Worth, so helping children to own their Inherent Worth must be helpful in reducing the possibility of developing mental health issues. If Inherent Worth is the key to recovery, it must also be the key to prevention—and that's what I wish I'd learned in prenatal class!

KEY TAKEAWAYS

It is not your child's job to make you happy. Your child already has a job: to be a child.

- Don't link your happiness to your child's behavior or achievements.
- Be very honest about your reasons for enrolling your child in activities. Is there any chance that you are living vicariously through your child? Do you ever ask your child to perform for others as a way of deriving pleasure yourself?

The best way to help your child is to reconnect with your own true self.

- Give yourself permission to work on your own well-being for the well-being of your family.
- Begin to notice every time you look for your worth outside yourself, such as checking how many "likes" your recent Facebook post received, or seeking the approval of a boss, a partner, or even your children. Becoming aware of this tendency is the first step to increasing your happiness.
- Adopt the mantra "My worth is inherent" (or "absolute," "a done deal," "intrinsic," or any other wording you prefer) and remind yourself as often as possible throughout the day.

Chapter Two

Is There a Problem with Self-Esteem?

> *"Work at not needing approval from anyone and you will be free to be who you truly are."*
> –Nachman of Bratslav

There are shelves of books about the importance of self-esteem to a child's healthy development, and few would dispute that high self-esteem correlates with "success" and happiness, but I want to point out a significant difference between self-esteem and what I refer to as Inherent Worth (IW). Our children will thrive if their self-esteem derives from their understanding of their Inherent Worth, but they may run into trouble if their self-esteem is built on their achievements and external validation. This chapter will explain the significance of having the right kind of self-esteem.

Inherent Worth Defined

Inherent Worth is the idea that everyone has the same worth—infinite worth—by virtue of just being, regardless of race, religion, gender, health, status, wealth, or any other external factor. We all have the same unlimited potential, despite our differing circumstances and abilities. Inherent Worth doesn't depend on what we accomplish or don't accomplish; it is always there no matter what. We don't have to earn it and there's nothing we can do to taint it. It is a constant throughout our lives, though we may not be aware of it at all.

Your Inherent Worth is absolute. Your IW just is. It doesn't depend on what you achieve or don't achieve. It is neither changeable nor variable. It's impossible for anyone to be worth more than anyone else—understanding this yourself and helping children to understand this as they grow up will go a long way towards raising mentally healthy kids. Someone who is aware of his Inherent Worth will be:

- Nonjudgmental
- Non-blaming
- Loving
- Caring
- At peace with self and others
- Resilient
- Creative
- Kind
- Confident
- Passionate
- Grateful
- Positive

It is only when we lose sight of who we truly are that we are tempted to judge others and ourselves, blame others and ourselves, and live stressful, impoverished lives. Remembering the truth of our Inherent Worth, and owning it, is the way to a rich and happy life.

The Trouble with Self-Esteem

Self-esteem is the measure of our worth by our own estimation based on evidence, such as the approval of others or skills we've mastered. We need to earn it and so it depends on our achievements—on external factors. As such, it is variable, and can be lost if we fail to measure up to the standards we have set for ourselves or which others have set for us.

We feel good about ourselves when we master new skills or achieve a goal and that's terrific, but we need to know that we are no less worthy if we never achieve "success." When my granddaughter was four months old she learned to roll over and it gave her a tremendous sense of joy—finally being on the move! That joy is the joy we want our children to feel every day and the joy we ourselves would like to feel on a daily basis. It is our birthright to be joyful. However, my granddaughter's worth would be no less if she had never learned to roll over.

The trouble with self-esteem is that it can easily be lost. If we encourage children to earn self-esteem by doing praiseworthy things, they will replace their self-esteem with a sense of failure or guilt when they don't measure up. It is this loss of self-esteem that is so dangerous. In the same way that high self-esteem is linked to happiness and success, low self-esteem is linked to risky behavior, addictions, depression, and even suicide.

In high-achieving families, children may look at their parents, see their success, and measure themselves by it, thinking that they won't be able to have the same success. They put high expectations on themselves (or their parents put expectations on them) that they don't think they can meet and so self-esteem takes a hit.

The adolescent and teen years are particularly hazardous to self-esteem in that for the first time, kids are venturing outside of their parents' control and may experiment with things their parents do not approve of, which may lead to guilt feelings and attendant loss of self-esteem. Puberty can lead to a loss of self-esteem in many children because of the unpredictable schedule of physical changes and mood swings—it can be a minefield of physical and logistical challenges for preteens and teens. From acne on the face before a school dance, to clumsiness in a rapidly growing body, erections that pop up unexpectedly, and embarrassing blood stains on clothing, there are numerous potholes to derail self-esteem at this vulnerable time in their lives.

Here's the important point: **If you define your worth by your achievements, your appearance, or your composure, there is a risk that you'll believe you are worthless if you fail, if your appearance changes, or if you are embarrassed by circumstances.** The same applies to your children. Inherent Worth never changes, so being in touch with that is crucial to mental health and happiness.

Self-Esteem and Competition

It would be logical to think that winning a competition would boost self-esteem. Just being qualified to enter should do the same. This is not necessarily so. Self-esteem that is generated from climbing a ladder higher than someone else, such as winning a competition, getting a higher score on a test, or scoring more goals in a game, is a double-edged sword. It leads to the idea that people have *different* worth. Someone is always higher on the ladder than we are, and this can lead to subconscious feelings of not being good enough.

If you plan to enter your child into a competition because you think they have a good chance of winning and that it would be good for their self-esteem—think again. Winning a competition may come with a side order of doubt or even guilt. Did I really deserve to win? What happens if I don't win next time? Will anyone figure out that I cheated? Was someone else better but didn't get noticed? Now I must keep winning to keep my coach happy.

The temporary feeling of joy at winning can be replaced with ongoing doubts and concerns if there isn't a strong sense of the self-esteem that comes from knowing that everyone has the same Inherent Worth. With that clear knowledge, competitions and winning would be fun and without anxiety. Imagine what sports would be like if the participants were playing for the joy of it without the pressure of winning.

Children may believe that they are better than others if they are in a more advanced group at school or in sports, but the idea that they could be better opens the door to self-doubt. Similarly, being in the slower group can damage self-esteem, but makes no difference whatsoever to Inherent Worth.

Attempts to boost student self-esteem by giving ribbons for participation at school sports days or junior soccer tournaments haven't worked. Studies have shown that the school ribbons for participation have not enhanced self-esteem in students one iota. In fact, it has decreased it overall (Jonathan Fader PhD, *Psychology Today*, June 2018). Helping children to be aware of their Inherent Worth, rather than trying to help them build self-esteem, is the key. Then it won't matter which group they are in nor how well they perform in a competition, in a classroom, or on the soccer field.

Perils of Too Much Praise

How many of us do what we do to win approval from our bosses, peers, spouse, other family members, and even our children? When that approval is not forthcoming we beat ourselves up wondering what we did wrong or reminding ourselves that once again we failed.

It is important not to train children to be constantly looking outside themselves for approval, which will happen as long as they are trying to establish their own worth instead of being sure that they have all the worth they will ever need. We need to teach them to find approval within themselves. So, be careful with praise—we don't want to raise children who are praise-dependent. Having a strong sense of Inherent Worth is crucial in countering the tendency we have of looking for and finding evidence that our underlying negative beliefs are true.

How will I encourage my child if I don't use praise?

If your child brings a painting home from school, you might ask her about the painting—did she enjoy painting it? How did she decide which colors to use? How did it make her feel? Is she pleased with the result? What will she paint next time? These questions will help her to understand her own response to painting. Is this an activity that she enjoys? What are the aspects that are enjoyable? You'll learn a lot more about her and help her learn about herself as well. Helping her tune into her feelings about the painting will allow her to process her emotional responses to the painting. Perhaps she was frustrated that she couldn't get the proportions right or that she couldn't mix exactly the color she wanted. Feelings of frustration point to an underlying negative belief and this can be countered by reminding her that her Worth is Inherent—it doesn't depend on how well she paints. Perhaps she feels fantastic and the picture is exactly how she wanted it to turn out. Then she will be encouraged to continue exploring her creativity through art. It is important that children do the things they want to do because they want to do them—not because we want to live vicariously through our children and reap the rewards of having an artistic child prodigy.

Barbara Coloroso, in her book *Kids are Worth It!*, cautions parents to be neutral when children bring home report cards: "If you get excited about your child's performance, connecting his performance with his dignity and worth as a person, you are encouraging him to view mistakes as a negative reflection of himself; something to be denied or blamed on someone else."

Whether it is an A or a D, simply be curious. That way you'll help the child to understand his strengths and weaknesses without judging him. If we get excited when a child brings home a high grade, then we are giving the message that high grades make us happy and he may be tempted to hide papers that have poor grades. If we are neutral and accepting, he will feel comfortable sharing his mistakes as well as successes and will know that we are there to help and offer suggestions if he needs them.

Begin to notice all the times that you are tempted to use praise, and instead be curious. Don't stop cold turkey or your children might be confused but do see how often in a day you use praise automatically. By changing the emphasis from *your* reaction to a child's work to their own reaction to it, you'll be helping them figure out what they love to do, what are their strengths and their weaker points. You'll be helping them understand themselves better and they will be freed from the role of making you happy.

Subconscious Sabotage

It is possible to have self-esteem "on paper" based on our achievements, musical talent, athletic, or academic ability, but at the same time have a subconscious belief that we are unworthy or even worthless, stupid, unlovable, or any number of other beliefs. The subconscious beliefs will sabotage our happiness, and can even lead to addiction, depression, and other self-destructive behavior despite the self-esteem we *appear* to have.

In my own life, as an adult, I went to my doctor with depression and he failed to understand how I could possibly be depressed given that outwardly my life looked perfect! I had the house, the husband, two children, university degrees, and a job that I enjoyed. When I see that list, I recognize that my self-esteem based on these external successes should have been high, but the subconscious beliefs I had were preventing me from experiencing the happiness that might otherwise result. Understanding that our Worth is Inherent is the antidote to these subconscious negative beliefs.

CIRCLES AND LADDERS

In 2012, I attended a tribunal held in Vancouver by the Stephen Lewis Foundation. It put the Canadian government on trial for not doing enough to help African grandmothers who are raising their grandchildren because of the AIDS epidemic, which has wiped out children's parents—almost an entire generation—in sub-Saharan Africa. Several African grandmothers were on hand to present their case and the auditorium was filled with Canadian grandmothers who have developed a strong bond with them through a "grandmothers to grandmothers" campaign. One after the other, the African women presented their stories of the atrocious conditions and circumstances they face at home.

They told of crime, rape, and living in poverty trying to do the best for their grandchildren at a time in their lives when their own health needs require attention. One of the panelists was Gloria Steinem and she summed up the issue (and solution) in a single phrase: "We are a circle, not a ranking." The majority of government agencies and society in general is set up as the exact opposite—a ranking, not a circle.

On any ranking African grandmothers are at the bottom of the ladder. They are female, black, poor, unhealthy, old, and live in Africa—it isn't possible to be lower on the ladder than that. The power and

> resources that could help them are in the hands of people who are predominantly wealthy, healthy, white men, who live in the northern hemisphere—at the top of the ladder. We need to have a perspective in which as people of the world we are a circle—no one is higher than any other. All are equally worthy of respect. If that were the case, African grandmothers would be given the resources that they so desperately need.
>
> Our children need to grow up knowing that as people we are a circle not a ranking—in this way, the wrongs of the world will eventually be righted, and the world will face a bright future.
>
> *"It is clear that the way to heal society of its violence... and lack of love is to replace the pyramid of domination with the circle of equality and respect."*
> — Manitonquat

The ongoing quest for high self-esteem can inadvertently cause children to believe that they must earn their worth, and places undue stress on them to "succeed." Focusing children on their Inherent Worth, however, will lead to a mentally healthy outlook and much less stress.

The images of circles and ladders provide a way to visualize the problem that society has with its obsession on stacking people up on ladders rather than gathering them around a circle. Metaphorically, stepping off the ladder of achievements and into a circle of Inherent Worth is the way to achieve not only inner peace, but ultimately world peace.

Ways in which parents can enhance a child's awareness of their Inherent Worth are given in the next chapter.

KEY TAKEAWAYS

Self-esteem can be too easily lost. High self-esteem can be maintained if the source of it is internal—a deep-seated knowledge that a person's worth is inherent and unchangeable.

- ❖ Avoid using external evidence as a way of helping your child to increase self-esteem.
- ❖ Shift your attention to helping your children to understand that they have Inherent Worth that is constant.

Competition can be fun if the competitors know they have Inherent Worth.

- ❖ Winning and losing can both be stressful so competition is best undertaken when participants are confident in their Inherent Worth.
- ❖ Don't push your children into competitions unless they are excited about the fun of it.
- ❖ Make sure that you are not more interested in the outcome than your child!

❖ Check in with your child's feelings about winning or losing so that there are no lingering repercussions about the competition.

Be careful with praise.
❖ Notice how often you use praise without thinking.
❖ Be curious about the project, the game, the song, the picture, or whatever it is you are tempted to praise.
❖ Avoid using money or other rewards for grades or chores.

"We are a circle not a ranking" is a mentally healthy way to view our place in the world.

❖ Step off the ladder! This may take a leap of faith, but do take the time to think about what this would look like for your family.

Chapter Three

How to Help Children to Recognize and Own Their Inherent Worth (IW)

"I will never understand all the good that a simple smile can accomplish."
–Mother Teresa

In the previous chapters, I have made a case for the importance of knowing our IW and I've encouraged you to work on helping your children to know theirs. How can we do this? There are nine suggestions below, most easy and quick to implement. Try to incorporate as many as possible for best results. As with any new habit it takes about three weeks to solidify—it will be worth it to you and your children to persevere. Results may not be immediate, but these strategies build over time and need reinforcing frequently. You can download this list on a single page from my website to print out and keep handy for reference—www.anneandrew.com.

1. Teach by example — see ourselves and others as Inherently Worthy

One of the key suggestions that I will keep coming back to is that we teach best by example, and that our children, particularly when they are very young, look to us to see how to be in the world. They check to make sure our words and deeds are congruent. Consequently, if we want our children to know their IW and own it, one of the most important things we must do is to recognize the IW of every person we meet and treat each person accordingly. Ask yourself, is there a difference in the way I treat the custodian as opposed to the principal, or the office assistant as opposed to the doctor? Do we treat the person who calls to sell us something with contempt, or are we polite? Do we acknowledge everyone, even when they are aggravating, bureaucratic, or begging? Did we honk the horn when someone tried to merge in front of us on the highway or did we let them in with a smile? Did we look the other way when we walked past the man on the sidewalk with his upturned cap asking for money? We need to be consistent in our application of this rule—that everyone has IW—or our children will question their own IW and seeds of doubt will be sewn in their minds. If we belittle anyone or show a lack of reverence, then the whole notion of IW can be challenged, and likely will be. Even if our children didn't notice the time we were less than unconditionally respectful, if we are not consistent in applying this idea, they will eventually deduce that some people are worth more than others. This is the beginning of doubt and unhappiness. They'll get a sense that people are stacked up on a ladder of achievement, and that it's their duty to move up as high as they can for their parents to be happy.

Just as important as how we treat others is how we treat ourselves. Do we make time to care for ourselves, to meditate, eat healthy meals, exercise, and have fun? Or do we go full steam ahead at our jobs? Are we unable to spend time away from our children because we believe it's our place to be with them at all times? Even if it is not possible to trade babysitting with a friend long enough to have a quiet moment at an exercise class or at a café, you can let your children know that you are taking some time for yourself to meditate or stretch, read a book, make a healthy snack, or otherwise pamper yourself. Children need to know that there is something to look forward to in being an adult—it is not only chores and hard work. It sets a good example for them to see you taking time out for yourself. You may be thinking that you simply don't have the time for self-care, and that is certainly a huge challenge, but my point is that it is a priority, so give yourself permission!

When I was home with my children, I didn't allow time for myself, and I wish I had. I would have set a much better example for my children if I hadn't been constantly stressed, overworked, and irritable! The message I was giving them was that it was my job to take care of them and my own health didn't matter as much. I was inadvertently showing them that people have different worth, rather than that we all have the same IW. If we focus solely on our children, without taking care of ourselves, we may become resentful, and that gets in the way of love.

2. Smile.

When was the last time someone smiled at you? How did it feel? How do you feel when you smile at others? Have you ever smiled at someone across a crowded room and felt as if you've shared a moment that is precious?

A smile is the simplest gift of love that you can give and one of the most profound ways to acknowledge the IW of everyone. Smile at everyone you meet and don't forget your family members—it is infectious! Smiles can be given with no expectation that it will be returned, but it usually is. Think about how often you smile at your children in a day and then increase the dosage and the volume of your smile—it'll help them to know their IW. When things go wrong and life feels tough, it is easy to forget to smile, but our children are nourished by our smiles. Here are a few things smiles communicate to them:

- ❖ I love you
- ❖ I see you
- ❖ I accept you
- ❖ You are OK
- ❖ I'm OK
- ❖ You have Inherent Worth
- ❖ I have Inherent Worth
- ❖ We are connected

When we smile we release "happy" hormones (endorphins) that give us a sense of well-being, and we reduce cortisol, adrenaline, and even blood pressure. Challenge every member of your family to smile at everyone they meet for one day and report back about how those days went. I can guarantee that you'll all be reporting a pretty good day.

In his TED talk "The Hidden Power of Smiling," Ron Gutman shows that people who smile live longer, are more successful, and live more fulfilling lives than those who don't. He claims that a smile stimulates the same feel-good brain activity level as two thousand chocolate bars (which wouldn't feel so good if you ate them all at once) or being handed twenty-five thousand dollars in cash. That's amazing, considering how easily available, cost-free, quick, and silent smiling is. He also points out that it is very difficult to frown when someone is smiling at us—so true! Smiling at a grumpy child is likely to help that child feel better, and we'll also feel great because of the reduction of stress-inducing hormones and the increase of feel-good hormones that are released in the one doing the smiling.

Some years ago, I attended an awards evening in Vancouver called "The Courage to Come Back Awards." Awards were given to a number of people who had overcome obstacles to achieve success in their fields. One of the recipients of this award told her story. She had been homeless, living on the streets of Vancouver. She felt ashamed, and completely hopeless until one day, a passerby smiled at her. From this simple gesture a friendship began, and with that seed of hope this woman was able to get back on her feet, gain employment, and thrive. The smile that was offered to her gave her life back to her quite literally, so never underestimate the power of a smile.

We give our children life—the sure knowledge that they have IW—when we smile at them. Put a smiley face sticker on your fridge or on your cell phone to remind you to keep on smiling. You have no idea how many lives you might save and you'll feel great in the process!

3. Meditation or mindfulness.

Meditation involves turning inward and experiencing the self or the mind as extending beyond the confines of our bodies. It provides access to the serenity of our innermost selves. Some children may not have experienced this inner space much, because of the constant distraction of TV and video games, so having an opportunity for quiet reflection, and awareness of the present moment, is a great way of getting in touch with their IW.

When we meditate we discover, eventually, that we are in control of our thoughts, our thoughts are not in control of us, unless we give our thoughts that power. This is a very important realization. If we can observe our thoughts without jumping on the thought train, we become able to dismiss unpleasant thoughts. What a gift to be able to do this! By learning to monitor our thoughts we can intercept those that are coming from our negative beliefs and use them to heal and transform those beliefs at their origin.

There is a huge body of scientific evidence to show that meditation and mindfulness are healthy practices for us to engage in. Brain science shows that it can reduce stress, ease tension, improve mood, and enhance virtually every aspect of our lives (such as research by Elizabeth Hoge at the Center for Anxiety and Traumatic Stress Disorders and Moynihan et al. *Neuropsychobiology, 2013*). The benefits are enormous—we must help our children develop these skills.

Children can learn to meditate and be mindful—mindfulness is now commonplace in many school districts and rightfully so. At my school, I instituted meditation for the children every week. We did this at the beginning of the day and all the teachers reported that the children were calmer and more receptive to their learning and more focused in their activities all morning.

With a guided meditation specialist, even the children who were diagnosed with ADHD were able to participate and their symptoms improved significantly in the short term. Children as young as those in grade two were able to focus using guided meditation for five minutes or even longer. Our grade six and seven students were meditating for ten to fifteen minutes each session.

I am certain that the meditation program that I instituted at the school was the single most beneficial part of the curriculum. That was confirmed to me when one of my former students informed me that she had used meditation to get through tough times as a teenager—she had been contemplating suicide—and was very grateful to me for allowing her the chance to learn meditation techniques.

If your child's school doesn't yet have a mindfulness program, be an advocate for one. Approach the school principal or counselors with evidence of the effectiveness of mindfulness on academic and psychological development and engage other parents in asking to make this kind of training available. Several schools in British Columbia (and many others across the U.S.) have adopted the MindUP program that was developed by the Goldie Hawn Foundation. Schools using the MindUP curriculum, which requires ten minutes three times a day, report increased academic achievement and decreased disruptive student behavior. Those are results that every school would like to have.

Implementing mindfulness at home

There are numerous books, CDs, apps, and websites dealing with how to meditate with children. I have listed a few in the "Resources" section (Appendix A) as a place to start.

Mindfulness for young children can be as simple as tracing a labyrinth on paper, dissolving a Lifesaver candy on the tongue for as long as possible, or keeping their eyes on a large letter, candle flame, or word, but they quickly become more sophisticated and can meditate for increasing lengths of time.

One parent I know has her children listen to guided meditations in the car on the way to and from school. Just be careful because driving and meditating don't go together, so be sure to use headphones yourself (listening to something else), or have your children use headphones so that you can drive safely!

Listening to a guided meditation at bedtime can be a peaceful way to end the day and prepare for a good sleep. Playing meditative music in the morning at breakfast before school will get the day off to a calm start. Mindfulness can be practiced at mealtimes, even with small kids, by focusing their attention on the colors on their plate, the smells and textures of the different foods, and how each mouthful feels. Mindful eating can increase the enjoyment of food as well.

4. Adopt a gratitude practice.

It is well-documented that gratitude has a positive effect on mood and it helps to counter depression. Every book about happiness has a section on gratitude. This is not a coincidence. Scientific studies by Robert Emmons and others have shown that grateful people are happier and have fewer episodes of depression. When we are being grateful, we are accessing the loving part of ourselves—not the part that is constantly criticizing us and generally putting us down. When we practice being grateful, we become aware of the abundance that is ours, thereby increasing our awareness of our IW. We help our children to feel their IW when we encourage them to express gratitude. That's why I highly recommend starting a gratitude practice within your family if you don't already have one.

Can you imagine if it were possible to stem the tide of increasing mental health problems in youth, just by adding a gratitude habit into our family life? Imagine if this simple, free, non-medicinal intervention could make the difference between plain sailing through the teen years, and difficulties with teen problems such as addictions, eating disorders, anxiety, and other maladies. Can we really afford not to try this?

Oprah is a vocal supporter of having a gratitude practice and keeps a gratitude journal. She has transformed her life and the lives of her many fans by doing so and by encouraging others to do the same. Studies have shown that writing gratitude down actually increases the positive effects.

Expressing gratitude is one way to bring us in the present moment, which is the best (and happiest) place to be. I have a friend who sometimes calls me in the middle of a panic attack. I ask her to look around and find five things to be grateful for in her immediate environment. This easy activity halts the panic attack in its tracks and brings her into the present by engaging all her senses to find those five things.

Be specific about what you are grateful for

Gratitude is a central value in most religious traditions. In Judaism, for example, there is a systematic way of expressing gratitude through blessings. There are blessing formulas for different types of food (depending on how it is grown), for rainbows and thunder, seeing a beautiful tree, welcoming different holidays and seasons, for rain, for dew, and a myriad more. There is a tradition of saying one hundred blessings a day. This prescription is a way to recognize the extraordinary in the ordinary and to elevate the ordinary to a higher plane. In response to this tradition, my friend Danny Siegel, author and poet, wrote his own version of one hundred blessings—one hundred things he is grateful for that can inspire each of us to write our own one hundred blessings. I use his poem as an example of how to make our gratitude specific. Danny includes such things as "laughter shared with a friend," "the smell of cut grass," and "our hearing hearts."

By being specific, we focus our attention on the beauty of the world around us, of good people and kind acts. That focus keeps us present, grateful, and happy. We can't at the same time be moaning and complaining—falling into negative ways of thinking. Parents that I have worked with and who have instituted gratitude practice report that their children whine less. That's a blessing!

When I asked my students what they were grateful for, the answers were limited to some variation of "my family, my pets, the world, my health, and my friends." They listed the things they thought I wanted to hear. However, I doubt that most of them were terrifically grateful to their parents on a morning on which they would rather have stayed in bed than been brought to an extra session of school. I would always offer my own gratitude, which I would make very specific and detailed. At one of our evening classes I had to drive across the bridge from Vancouver to Richmond, and in the winter, there would often be a magnificent sunset. Then I would offer gratitude "for the orange tones of the sunset contrasting with the black silhouette of the mountains," or "the pattern of clouds that were tinged by the colors of the sunset." By demonstrating specific gratitude in this way, I encouraged them to observe their world more closely—to look at it with a sense of wonder. Gradually, they too offered specific things that they were grateful for: "the sunlight on the trees," "the smell of the flowers in the garden," "good things to eat," "smiles," and our rounds of gratitude would go on for a long time! This practice helped them to notice all the amazing things in the world and it changed their perception from one of entitlement to one of abundance.

How to develop a family gratitude habit:

There is no cookie cutter gratitude habit that will work for all families, so be creative and come up with your own unique version that fits your particular family. Parents sometimes ask if their children are likely to cooperate. I tell them that gratitude feels good, promotes calm, peace, happiness, and present awareness, so even older children like the results and are likely to enjoy these sessions. You know them best, so if you think your child will be resistant, simply express your own gratitude while they are around and be sure to tell them whenever you are grateful to them for something they said or did or simply for being part of your life.

Here are a few questions for you to consider:

1. Decide when?
    - Bedtime—A gratitude habit at bedtime can significantly improve sleep—what a bonus!
    - After school
    - Dinner time
    - Movie night
    - While walking the dogs (my personal favorite!)
    - Thanksgiving or other family occasions

2. Decide where?
    - In the car between activities
    - On the way to or from school
    - In bed
    - At the dinner table
    - Around a campfire

3. Decide how?
    - How many things should each person be grateful for? Consider using categories: something beautiful; something kind that someone did; something I was happy I was able to do.

- Will there be some ritual around this—such as passing a feather or a "talking stick" (a First Nations tradition of passing a carved stick from person to person as each person shares a story or an opinion in a discussion), or lighting a candle, or putting a quarter in a box for each gratitude, or recording it on a piece of paper or in a journal?
- Will each person take a turn? Who goes first? I suggest having an adult go first to begin with to demonstrate how to be specific.
- Will this be one child with one parent or the whole family?
- How often? Daily, weekly, yearly (birthdays, Thanksgiving, etc.)?
- Will everyone begin with "I'm grateful for..."? Or is there some other phrase you'd prefer to use?

Other occasions could be at birthdays before blowing out the candles—each person tells the birthday child what they love about him or her, or at a weekly family dinner or in the car after a sports practice. It is a way of inviting closeness and connection and finding out more about each other in the process.

A few recommendations:
- Have an adult go first to demonstrate.
- Be specific when giving examples to encourage a sense of wonder.
- Adopt your own gratitude habit—perhaps a journal—as always, we teach best by example.
- Be genuine. Children know when they are being manipulated.

If every parent and teacher would add "gratitude" to their "to do" or "to be" list, the world would quickly become a much happier place.

5. Look at your child with wonder

Once we are aware that everybody has IW that cannot be lost even when they misbehave, it becomes easier to see that IW in them. One of the best ways we can help our children to recognize their IW is by seeing it in them every day. When we look at our children as if seeing them for the first time, and see past their imperfections, we notice the miracle that they are. Try to see your child as you saw him on the day he was born. This is to look at a child with love. They will feel that love and know that they have IW even if they just pulled the dog's tail, poured water over a sibling's head, or failed a test at school—none of that alters their IW, and we must see them as whole, complete and totally worthy at all times.

There is a wonderful term coined by Abraham Joshua Heschel: "Radical amazement." I love the idea this conjures up for me of the surprise and delight that can be experienced when we look at anything and everything with fresh eyes. Looking at our children this way reminds us and them of the incredible beauty of who they truly are. As Heschel said:

> Our goal should be to live life in radical amazement.... Get up in the morning and look at the world in a way that takes nothing for granted. Everything is phenomenal; everything is incredible; never treat life casually. To be spiritual is to be amazed.

6. Listen well

When our children have something to say to us, we must listen to them carefully. This means giving them our full attention. If there is something competing for that attention we need to turn it off or put it away—cell phones are the main culprit these days, but the TV or our work can also get in the way. A recent study (AVG technologies, June 2015) has shown that children whose parents are constantly on their cell phones think they are unimportant. Their sense of self-esteem plummets. The opposite is true. Focusing your attention on them when they need you is a sure way of indicating to them you recognize their IW. Obviously, it is not possible to listen with rapt attention to every babble that the newly talking toddler mutters but taking the time as often as possible to do so will help them own their IW.

One of the exercises that I like my workshop participants to experience is a deep listening activity. They pair up and each pair then spends several minutes making, and keeping, eye contact with each other. This is remarkably difficult to do—we are not used to engaging with another person with this level of intensity, and it makes us feel uncomfortable. Even married partners report that this degree of intimacy is rare in their relationships. The question is why is this so hard? I think the answer is that when we look into another person's eyes we are seeing deeply into that person and seeing our true self reflected—we have an aversion to being truly *seen*. It is almost as if we feel naked.

Getting back to the exercise: The pair then alternates listening and speaking on a topic. There are several experiences in play—being listened to (rare indeed!); engaging intimately;

and listening to another. It is a powerful experience, but one that is worth having for a number of reasons:

- It helps us to understand how much closer we can be to our family members and others—we actually resist this kind of intimate connection;
- When we are that engaged in the relationship between us, it is possible to listen well—what usually passes for listening is simply hearing the words without connecting; and
- It helps us to recognize our own and another's Inherent Worth.

Find out what your comfort level is with looking into another's eyes and overcome the tendency to want to withdraw and look away. You'll be amazed at the results—your children (or your partner) will know that they have your ear (literally) and will be able to share their feelings and connect with you on a much deeper level than previously.

7. Use the mantra "Your worth is not established by...(fill in the blanks)."

When your child comes home from school with a glum expression on his face and you realize that he didn't get the outcome he was hoping for—he didn't win his race or did poorly on a spelling test—you can remind him that "your worth is not established by the report card you bring home, nor by how many goals you score, nor by how well you can play the piano. Nothing alters the fact that you have IW. Your IW is a done deal and it can never be lost."

My husband and I have fun with this—we tease each other. For example: "My worth is not established by having the dishes done before you get home;" "my worth is not established by being home on time;" "my worth is not established by having the lawn pristine, nor by how well I fold the laundry." I'm sure you'll enjoy coming up with these! These are playful reminders that if we are upset for any reason, it is not for the reason we think it is, but because we have forgotten our IW and instead believe that we are flawed in some way.

8. Be careful with praise

This was discussed in Chapter Two, but I'll reiterate it here for completeness.

Many parents and teachers believe that it is important to praise children for everything they do. This has gotten rather out of hand and has resulted in a generation of praise-dependent adults. If children are praised for every little thing they do, they may wonder if they have done something wrong when praise is not forthcoming (as it is unlikely to be when they enter the workforce). They may even do things to receive the praise, rather than because they want to do them for themselves.

Recently, there have been parenting articles and books suggesting that it is better to praise the *effort* rather than the achievement. This is a big step in the right direction, but I would argue that this can still lead to praise-dependency. A good strategy is to be curious rather than to have a knee-jerk praising response. Instead of praising a child's performance in her soccer game, ask her if she enjoyed playing. Ask about the process. Which drills helped her the most? How did her teammate know to pass the ball at just the right moment? How long did it take for the team to gel? Did she ever feel like giving up? Does she enjoy playing in the rain and getting muddy? Are there some teams she enjoys playing more than others? What makes playing soccer fun?

When a child senses your sincere interest in what she is doing, that acts as encouragement and helps her to sort her own feelings around her activities. She will learn what it is that she really enjoys doing. Keeping in mind that each child has IW is the important thing here and will protect us from being too wrapped up in our child's successes and failures.

9. Just Be!

Kick back. Relax. Have fun. Unplug from technology. Reclaim a day of rest. Decompress. Take time out from your busy schedules to be together and reconnect as a family. Put on some music and dance. Go for a walk in the rain—taking time to be in nature has been shown to enhance a sense of well-being and is a great way to keep a child's sense of wonder intact. Fly a kite!

Doing nothing together might be the greatest gift you can give your family and it will be one that you won't regret on your death bed! Aim for one day a week, but even part of a day may help to recharge your batteries. The Danish have perfected this technique and have given it a name, "*hygge*," which has gained interest around the world because of Denmark's standing as one of the happiest nations on earth. By allowing this free downtime, you'll be sending the clear message to children that life is a joy, something to be treasured and they will have the time they need to connect with you.

KEY TAKEAWAYS

There are ways to help children (and ourselves) experience their Inherent Worth directly—these include:

- ❖ Expressing gratitude
- ❖ Meditating or being mindful
  - ♦ Be an advocate for mindfulness programs in schools

Indirectly, children become aware of their IW when parents:

- ❖ Smile at them
- ❖ Look at them with wonder
- ❖ Listen well
- ❖ Model awareness of the IW of themselves and everyone else

Praise-dependency can be avoided by helping children to understand their own feelings around the things they do rather than using our praise as an automatic reaction.

- ❖ Ask about your child's activities to help them sort out their feelings about the things they do.

So, there you have it. Inherent Worth fully accepted and embraced will change your life and that of your family members and friends. As with many seemingly "simple" ideas it can be difficult to fully grasp as previous "ways of being" assert and reassert themselves. In Part Two I will explain why it is so difficult for us to accept and own our Inherent Worth and what to do about it.

PART TWO

Unconditional Love: A Parent's Guide

Chapter Four

Do We Really Know How to Love Unconditionally?

"When a child is most unlovable is when that child needs loving the most."

–Rachel Aronin Wasserman

In Part One, we looked at the importance of a child's Inherent Worth in maintaining mental health. In this section, we'll look at how our sense of our Inherent Worth gets lost as we develop negative beliefs about ourselves in early childhood. These negative beliefs act as barriers to parents giving love and to children receiving love, so it is crucial that parents understand how they form and what can be done about them.

"Hey, wait a minute," you may be thinking, "of course I love my children unconditionally!"

I know I thought that—that is until my daughter went off the rails as a teenager in a dramatic way. The way back for our family was by learning to love unconditionally. We learned it the hard way and I don't want that to happen to you.

We discovered that although we thought we were a loving, caring family, and certainly anyone who knew us would have agreed, our parenting was largely fearful making unconditional love virtually impossible. We had worries about our children's futures, and expectations of what that should look like for each of them. We felt we needed to shape them into fine humans rather than simply to accept them as they are. The good news is that it is possible with a few simple techniques, to learn to love *without fear* and to become more effective parents as a result.

At this point it will be useful for you to take the quiz (Appendix B) to self-assess your parenting—is it love-based or fear-based? Record your score and return to this point. You may be surprised at the result, but don't worry, most of us are far more fear-based in our thinking and actions than we are aware. Awareness is a big step in the right direction and you are reading this book so that you can make a shift to love! You'll retake the quiz at the end of Chapter Nine.

All You Need is Love

In the theory of "Maslow's hierarchy of needs" (Saul McLeod, SimplyPsychology.org), love comes right after physical needs and safety. We all know intuitively that children need love to thrive; in fact, we all do. Without question, we love our children—just think back to the day they were born or the day they arrived in our families if they were adopted. We ached with love for them.

The rush of love that you feel when a child is born (under typical circumstances) can be completely overwhelming. Childbirth is one of those times in our lives when some people report having a spiritual experience. That doesn't always happen, but the unconditional love for this new tiny human can be immense, and this is certainly one of the few times in our lives when the idea of unconditional love can be fully comprehended. When my first child was born, I was completely unprepared for the wave of love for my baby that engulfed me—it was so unexpected, so powerful, and so complete.

But there's a problem:

Parenting is a twenty-four-hour job, 365 days a year. Parents get tired and grumpy. There's a lot of fear around parenting—"Are we doing it right?"—or worry about what the future might bring. Children grow up and develop personalities of their own. We may have expectations of them that they do not meet. We may feel embarrassment or shame if they behave in ways we don't like. When they get older they may even tell us they hate us. Have you had that experience? When problems happen, particularly as the teen years approach, it can be difficult to like our children at times. Unconditional love is a challenge under these circumstances. We do, of course, have glimpses of it when our children are sleeping or look at us with their innocent eyes.

In his book *The Childhood Roots of Adult Happiness*, Edward Hallowell states that "the unconditional love of one adult in a child's life is the best inoculation against emotional distress." He goes on to say that the love must be felt by the child and not just offered by the adult. This is an important point and one to which I will return. There are, therefore, some crucial considerations if we can learn to love unconditionally:

1. Your child's mental health and happiness.
2. You'll have a better chance of avoiding the emotional (and financial) cost of having a problematic teenager.
3. Your own happiness will increase as a result of removing your barriers to love.

What is Unconditional Love?

So, let's establish what we mean by "unconditional love." When I ask parents for a definition of unconditional love, the question is often met with silence until I begin to prompt a little. Most parents genuinely believe that unconditional love is a given, and that they love their kids unconditionally, so being asked the question takes them by surprise—no one wants to admit that they find it difficult to love unconditionally.

A typical definition would be:

- ❖ Love that is given freely with no strings attached—just because.
- ❖ There is no expectation of being loved in return.
- ❖ There is no expectation of any achievement or standard of behavior.

I'd like to add:
- ❖ Unconditional love is experienced when someone who knows their Inherent Worth sees the Inherent Worth of another.
- ❖ It can be felt when we remove the barriers that block our awareness of it.
- ❖ It is automatic when a person is operating from a loving place rather than a fearful one.
- ❖ We can only extend love when we love ourselves.

Our job as parents is to initiate our children into knowing what love really is.

And, Diederik Wolsak offers a marvelous definition:

- ❖ Love is the joyful acceptance of what *is*. This might be a bit of a head-scratcher right now, but think about it as you read the book.

Is it Love or Bargaining?

What passes for love in many families is really bargaining. If you do this I'll do that—"I'll feed you and drive you to school if you clean your room, give me a hug at night, and tell me you love me and don't bring home any Ds." Of course, it is ridiculous to think that this kind of bargain is arranged, agreed upon, or spoken in any way, but many of our relationships rest on hidden agendas or subconscious agreements—bargains that we may not even be aware of.

Bargaining in a parent-to-child relationship can be a comfortable arrangement until one partner is not willing to keep their end of the bargain. The teen years in particular can put a strain on the notion of unconditional love, because the bargain begins to look quite different. Pushing boundaries and a changing level of demonstrable love from a child to a parent can feel threatening to the parent. Teen behavior can be outrageous at times, more difficult to predict or control, and may embarrass a parent in such a way that the parent's own worth is challenged, and so love is threatened.

Any bargain places conditions on love. Here are some typical ones:

1. **I need you to establish my worth.**
This happened in our household and is common to many. Subconsciously, I gave the message: "I'm not sure of my own worth, so I need you to provide it for me by making me look good." This is unlikely to work and the exact opposite can happen instead! The solution for my family was for me to reclaim *my* Inherent Worth to free my children of having to provide my worth for me.

2. **I don't have enough love so I need you to provide it for me.**
Similar to needing a child to establish a parent's worth, some parents need their children to provide love. Children will inevitably fail to make their parents happy all the time and will develop beliefs about themselves that they are inadequate or not good enough.

3. **Love equals good grades.**
It seems natural to get excited about a child's achievements, but by doing so, parents give the message that these things make them happy. The child may then deduce that poor

marks or failure will make their parents unhappy. Children may even begin to equate love with approval, and approval with achievement—that love is conditional on good grades.

4. Unconditional obligation isn't love.

Unconditional love may also be mistaken for unconditional obligation. If I pay for my neighbor's broken window, or bail out a teenager from jail—is it love or obligation? If resentment is involved in any way, then it is not being done out of love. The agreement then might be, "I'll love you as long as you don't get into trouble and embarrass me." It is worth pondering if there are any circumstances under which you would not love your child if you are totally honest!

5. Codependent negative beliefs.

It gets even more interesting when we consider the subconscious beliefs of parents and children and how they feed each other. My own negative belief that "I'm a bad parent" demanded evidence that my daughter subconsciously provided, and her belief that she is "not good enough" was fed by my reactions to her behavior. The key to opening the channels for unconditional love, which supplied the healing we both needed, was to clear these and other negative beliefs that we both held.

Bargaining happens on a much deeper subconscious level as well: I may need my child to establish my worth because deep down I feel worthless, and I may also need that child to fail at it to bring me evidence for the belief that I'm a bad parent. At the same time, a child may need to excel to get love from a parent and may need to fail at it to gain evidence for a deep-seated belief that they are not good enough. This is a "waltz" that they do together, and which many families get locked into. This idea will be explored in more detail in this and the next two chapters.

Why is Unconditional Love So Rare?

We can't truly love another if we don't first love ourselves.

> *"I don't trust people who don't love themselves and tell me, 'I love you.'....There is an African saying which is: Be careful when a naked person offers you a shirt."*
> –Maya Angelou

We can't give something that we don't have. If we want to have a loving relationship with our spouse or kids, we have to fall in love with ourselves first.

At one of my talks on unconditional love, a mother told me that her young daughter had asked her, "Mommy, who do you love the most—me or you?" That mother had a difficult time answering her. She said, "I love you to the moon and back, but if I didn't love myself, I wouldn't be able to love you, so I love me just as much!" That's such a beautiful but remarkably uncommon sentiment.

Most of us don't actually love ourselves at all. Unconditional love is rare because of this.

For us to love our children, we must first love ourselves. This begs the question: Why don't we love ourselves?

The simple answer is that we have barriers to love—in the form of *negative beliefs*! Our barriers develop in early childhood and most of us are still walking around with these firmly in place.

Negative Beliefs

We all have a number of negative beliefs. You may be aware of them if they feed negative self-talk such as, "I don't belong" or "I'll never be good enough." Or they may be subconscious and you don't know they are there at all. Most of us have a subconscious belief that we are guilty—even though we may not consciously be aware of it. If a person in authority calls attention to something bad that someone has done, we will immediately feel guilty, even though it had nothing to do with us. Have you ever felt guilty going through customs, despite having nothing to declare?

Once we have one of these beliefs, whether it is conscious or subconscious, we see our world from the perspective of that belief. We find evidence to support it. If we believe we're bad, we'll behave in ways that prove that we are. If we subconsciously feel worthless, we'll notice every time that someone treats us that way, but we may not notice all the times people treat us kindly. Each time we collect evidence we bolster the belief and make it stronger.

The following diagram shows how beliefs lead to thinking—they feed negative self-talk and cause us to think we see evidence for the beliefs in the situations around us. Those thoughts lead to uncomfortable feelings, such as anger or any of the feelings listed in Appendix C. The resulting behavior strengthens the belief.

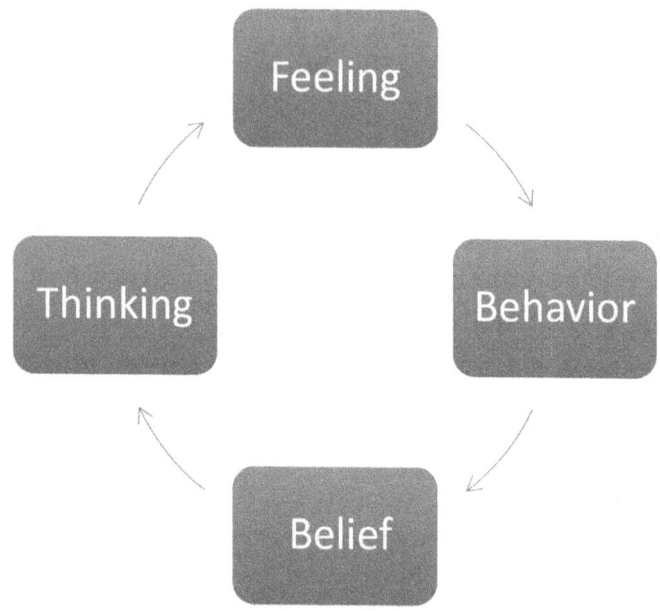

Figure 1. Belief Cycle

You may have noticed that some of your behaviors are repetitive in nature. You may consider them character traits—such as pessimism, perfectionism, messiness, contrariness, argumentativeness, submissiveness, and countless others. A pattern of behavior can develop from a single pivotal experience between birth and age eight. These pivotal experiences need not be particularly traumatic, though they may seem so to a child.

So How Do These Beliefs Develop?
Negative beliefs form in early childhood (between birth to age eight) at the stage of life in which children are egocentric. Children try to understand the world from an egocentric

standpoint (Violet Kalyan-Masih, 1973) so they deduce that they are responsible for the things that happen around them and they will make up beliefs about themselves to explain events. These beliefs are never true.

Our children develop negative beliefs about themselves as they experience life, as they interact with family and friends, teachers and coaches. They believe subconsciously that they are bad, stupid, guilty, worthless, that there is something wrong with them and that they are, therefore, unlovable—that's who they think they are.

Let me tell you the story of how one of my own negative beliefs formed.

Pirates!

When I was four or five, I was on a summer holiday on the coast, with my mom and dad and my brother. This particular day, we were taken to the dock, where there was a great big wooden galleon. I could hardly believe my luck that we were going to go on board and sail away! I held tightly onto my mom's hand as we climbed the steep gangplank, and the sailor at the top helped me jump down onto the deck. When all the passengers had assembled, the captain told us, "This is the Hispaniola, and we will be heading to Treasure Island. There are gold coins there, buried somewhere beneath the sand."

Off we sailed and soon Treasure Island came into view. The ship docked and we disembarked down the same wooden gangplank onto a white sandy beach. My brother and I began digging with our hands in the fine sand. I was deeply engrossed in hunting for the treasure when, all of a sudden, three men jumped out of the bushes beside the beach—pirates—and they were pointing their guns at us! Well, I was terrified, and my hands flew into the air. Everyone started to laugh. I looked around and realized that I was the only one with my hands up and all the people on the beach were looking at me, laughing. I grabbed hold of my mom's legs, moved around behind her, and hid, burying my face in the folds of her skirts, wanting to become invisible. A feeling of acute embarrassment engulfed me—how could I have been so stupid as to think the pirates were real?

As a result of my encounter on the beach on Treasure Island, "I am stupid" became one of my core beliefs. I carried that around with me for nearly fifty years! Acute embarrassment is a familiar feeling for me—it crops up whenever I do something that I consider "stupid." I made up that I was stupid, found all kinds of evidence to support it, but it was never true. "Stupid" is simply a label that does not serve me. The result of this belief was twofold:

1. I tried to cover up my belief that I was stupid by being a high achiever—this condemned me to a life of constant stress (until I challenged the belief).
2. It got in the way of love, resulting in chronic depression. In my four-year-old mind, no one could possibly love a stupid girl.

My experience with the pirates illustrates two key points:

1. **We can't prevent our children from developing these beliefs.** My parents had no idea that I would be traumatized by that outing. Should we have stayed home instead? Of course not! What we *can* do is keep reminding our children of their Inherent Worth, and we can model our understanding of our own.
2. **The beliefs children make up are not true.** It is so clear that the belief I made up was wrong. People weren't laughing at a stupid girl, they were laughing because I looked so cute with my hands in the air and a shocked expression on my face.

Looking back at figure 1, the thought is: "people are laughing at me because I'm stupid"; the feeling is "acute embarrassment"; the behavior is "hiding behind my mom," which gave me more evidence of my belief that "I'm stupid." Subsequently, I would act in ways that would bring proof of being stupid, and which would give me a feeling of acute embarrassment—a familiar feeling throughout my life. Now, if I feel embarrassed, I immediately know that it is because my core belief has been triggered and I can simply remind myself that it is not true, and then the feeling will fade. When you heal an old belief, a barrier to the awareness of love comes down.

Barriers to Love

Negative beliefs get in the way of unconditional love. Here's how it works:

- ❖ If I believe I'm not good enough then I'll think subconsciously that my love is not good enough or that I don't have enough love. I will need to strike a bargain with a partner or child to provide love for me, so my love will be conditional on them loving me back.
- ❖ If I believe I'm worthless or incomplete, I may need my child to establish my worth for me, by achieving "success." That child will learn that love is conditional on achievement.
- ❖ Our negative beliefs are our "hot buttons" or triggers. I'm likely to get angry if someone treats me in an offhand way—perhaps a shopkeeper doesn't smile at me or seems to serve me grudgingly. If my belief that I am worthless is triggered, feelings are aroused that are the same feelings that occurred when the beliefs were generated in early childhood. This results in behavior that is unloving. When we tackle our negative beliefs we disable our hot buttons.
- ❖ We project our negative beliefs on others when we judge them. We will be judgmental of others for the things we dislike about ourselves. The judgments we have of others are wonderful clues to some of the most deeply held and most fervently projected beliefs we have. We don't want to acknowledge that we have these beliefs. When judging another, be aware that one of your negative beliefs has been exposed. There is

tremendous resistance to this idea, but when you judge you'll find out who you think you are. When we judge a child, we add barriers to a loving relationship and may feed his negative beliefs (unless he has a strong sense of his Inherent Worth and then the judgment will not affect him). Being judgmental is not loving—it is fear-based.

Negative beliefs block love from being *received* as well. When I was working as a school principal, I worked closely with a dear colleague. One day I was in his office and it was soon after a former student had committed suicide. Sadly, there had been a few similar tragedies. Sometimes my colleague needed to vent. On this occasion, he made fists and yelled, "Don't our children know we love them?"

Well, unfortunately, the answer is no. They don't always. It isn't that we don't tell them. It isn't that they can't hear us say the words. It's that they don't believe the words. Children who are in a lot of trouble—it is easy to see—believe that they are unlovable. They know what they had to do to feed their addictions; they cannot imagine that it is possible for anyone to love them. It is impossible for them to believe that they have Inherent Worth. Even young children develop a subconscious belief that they are not lovable and can't receive the love that is being offered.

Any child who has a strong belief that he is not good enough, bad, unworthy or any other belief, will find it difficult to let love in. That child will think, consciously or unconsciously, "If only you knew how bad, unworthy, unlovable (fill in the blanks) I am, you would not choose to love me. You have to say you love me because you are my parent, but I can't believe it."

One of the formative experiences for my daughter was the time I was late picking her up from ballet. Ironically, I had just been prescribed a new antidepressant and it made me drowsy. I had fallen asleep after dropping her off for her preschool ballet class, and I didn't wake up until the phone rang and it was the ballet teacher asking me to come and pick her up! Of course, my daughter was distraught by the time I got there, and she had the thought that she must be worthless or her mother would have picked her up on time. In subsequent years, her recurring self-talk was fed by the belief "I'm worthless," based on that memory of me being late picking her up from ballet. She was merciless in picking up evidence for her belief, which eventually led to a number of negative behaviors that were resistant to change.

Dr. Joe Dispenza, in his book *You are the Placebo,* suggests that these beliefs are hardwired into our brains by a process of repeating thought patterns. We etch our traumatic experiences into our brains neurologically, and into our bodies chemically as emotions, so our thoughts and feelings are actually based on memories of the past. He also shows that due to neuroplasticity, the brain can regenerate and change these neural pathways if thoughts are changed at their source. Based on his work, brain science supports the concept that our thoughts and feelings are linked to past memories—our negative beliefs were generated in the past, and supply the same thoughts and feelings that we felt in the originating trauma, whenever they are activated or "triggered" in the present.

Removing Barriers to Love Changes Negative Behavior Patterns

The diagram (Fig. 1) clearly shows that if we want to change a behavior pattern, we must change the negative belief that is driving that behavior. This is a completely different approach than behavior modification and other methods that focus on behavioral *symptoms*, rather than on the *cause*.

Let me tell you about one of my recurring behavior patterns—a behavior I was not proud of and desperately wanted to change. For many years as a child I would get upset and yell at my parents. It didn't happen often, but there were things they did (or didn't do) that triggered me to yell. As motivated as I was to change, as hard as I tried, and as carefully as I went through the steps that I thought would lead to change—admitting I'd done something wrong, feeling bad about it, and saying sorry to my parents—the final step of making the change so that it didn't happen again never happened. I was relying on willpower and that just doesn't work in the long term.

Then came my daughter's problems and I started working with Diederik Wolsak, who developed the Choose Again Six-Step Process. I applied his Six-Step Process to a recent incident I had, in which yelling was involved. Because of my ongoing rush of angry feelings, Diederik guided me to follow those feelings into an early childhood memory. It didn't take me long to find myself in my old house, in the kitchen with my mom. I was about three. I was drawing a picture on a page of my new scrapbook with some crayons and was very pleased with myself. I wanted to show her what I'd done. "Mom! Mom! Momomomom!" She didn't look up—just kept on chopping onions, creating a heap at the side of the chopping board. Hadn't she heard me? Was she ignoring me? My three-year old self was crushed.

I looked at Diederik. "Oh, my God!" I suddenly realized that way back then I had interpreted my worth to be rather less than a heap of chopped onions! I'd been spending my life trying to establish my worth, whether in seeking my mother's approval, or pursuing it at universities, but what I now understood was that my worth was there all along. That realization was a huge breakthrough for me. I could see that seemingly innocuous episodes from my childhood, whether being laughed at on Treasure Island or being ignored by my mother, had been hugely impactful to me throughout my life and that their negative impact needed to be undone.

I was able to see that my yelling came from a negative belief I held about myself that I am worthless. When I was able to remind myself of my Inherent Worth then the usual triggers ceased to work. I haven't yelled (the way I used to) in years. **So, healing a subconscious negative belief actually changes our behavior.** This is a key point because if we want to change our behavior, we have to tackle the *cause* of that behavior, which is the belief that triggered it. It stands to reason that a parent who yells cannot love unconditionally, and a child of a yelling parent is unlikely to feel loved, so fixing the yelling behavior is of primary importance. Unloving behaviors exhibited by parents such as anger, impatience, and many others can be fixed when parents tackle their negative beliefs.

The "Aha!" moment that I had a few years ago as I was figuring all this out is that the Choose Again Six-Step Process that Diederik devised actually tackles a different problem (my belief that "I'm worthless") than the one I thought I had (my yelling). It tackles the underlying *cause* of problem behavior and can therefore change the behavior that I want to change. The goal of the Six-Step Process is to reestablish innocence—to reconnect with that Inherently Worthy self, and so reaffirms the importance of IW as the antidote to our negative beliefs. It gives us a way to tackle our own negative behavior—which doubtless gets in the way of unconditional love.

Similarly, if we want to help our children to change their unwanted negative behaviors, we must not only reaffirm their Inherent Worth, which acts as the antidote to the negative beliefs that they may have, but we must also stop inadvertently feeding their negative beliefs to the best of our abilities. Blaming, shaming, guilting, and punishing our children need to stop—these serve only to worsen behavior and make long-term problems more likely. There are other, more subtle ways that we feed our children's negative beliefs. We give unloving messages unintentionally.

Removing barriers to love is the best way to clear the way for unconditional love and is an important strategy for preventing the development of self-loathing in children, which over time can lead to depression, addiction, and other problems.

A NOTE ABOUT DEPRESSION

Depression can be thought of as being due to feeling a lack of love (Diederik Wolsak). Since negative beliefs block our awareness of love, healing those beliefs will naturally relieve depression. This was the process by which I was able to conquer depression in my own life. Having been on antidepressants for years, it was remarkable how quickly my depression responded to the process of challenging my negative beliefs using the Six-Step Process. This has been shown to be the case over and over again by many of Diederik's clients. In simple terms then, healing my beliefs that "I'm stupid" and "I'm worthless" also lifted my depression!

SUICIDE PREVENTION BEGINS IN PRESCHOOL

Suicide can be a result of depression, and is one of the "side effects" listed on the packages of several antidepressants. As I have explained, young children (from birth to eight) develop the negative beliefs that can lead to self-loathing and depression, so by tackling these negative beliefs as children grow up, we are really preventing suicide. If we are to make a dent in this problem, which is particularly bad in the university environment, we must tackle it while children are young. Can we afford not to?

Practical Suggestions for Loving Your Children Unconditionally:

1. **Know Who Your Children Truly Are**
Our children are Inherently Worthy beings—we need to understand this about them and communicate it to them when they forget. How do we do this?

- **Consider your children as merely lent to you.** By having this mind-set, you separate your own process from theirs. You will no longer feel the need to have them complete you, nor will you expect them to behave in a certain way so that you don't look bad.
- **See them as Inherently Worthy.** Look at them with radical amazement as if seeing them for the first time. That's how love can be *felt* by a child.
- **Help them know themselves as Inherently Worthy too.** All the suggestions in Chapter Three will help with this.
- **Know that they are good enough as they are.** They have unlimited potential. It's not your job to shape them into something you want them to be. You don't have to send them to the best preschool or sign them up for music lessons so that they can get into law school later.
- **Redefine success as inner peace and happiness.** Isn't that what we all really want for our families? Take a look at the famous people who are rich, but miserable. How many executives reach the top of the ladder only to find themselves feeling empty and then searching

for something to fill that emptiness? Often, substance abuse is the result, but some become spiritual "seekers" and wonder why they previously didn't know the joy of inner peace. Happiness is not something that is taught in schools and western society has promoted consumerism and entertainment as ways to fill the void. Your children can grow up knowing that there is more to life than money and power.

2. Notice When Your Negative Beliefs are Getting in the Way
Have an honest look at yourself to determine if your negative beliefs (that go against the concept of IW) have influenced your parenting decisions, getting in the way of love.

- **Don't need your child to make you happy.** You don't need them to be your pride and joy. When you free them of this responsibility you free them to just be kids, which is their only job. If you have a negative belief that love is limited or that happiness comes from outside, then you might subconsciously be relying on your child for your happiness.
- **Don't overprogram—children need more time to play.** Play is the work of children (Dr. Shimi Kang's book *The Dolphin Parent* and Dr. Peter Gray's book *Free to Learn*). It is a crucial component in developing their academic and social abilities as well as life skills, and it helps them discover their passions. Overprogramming may be due to a parent fearing that their child won't measure up on some scale if they don't have extra

talents. It can also be a response to a lack of confidence in parenting by involving "experts" such as a drama coach, dance instructor, art teacher, or sports coach instead. It is unnecessary and unhealthy for children to spend their childhood preparing for university or a professional sports career. Relax—this really will be OK!

- ❖ **Don't have expectations of how you want them to be.** You are likely to be disappointed if you do. If you are currently pushing a child to practice piano, or to train hard to be a gymnast or baseball player, consider if you have any beliefs that may be driving this agenda. For this you must be extremely honest with yourself. You may well be tempted to live vicariously through a child, as I was.

> When Serena Williams' daughter was born, the bookmakers got busy placing bets on whether the child would eventually become a Wimbledon champion. This kind of external pressure and unnatural attention may rob a child of her ability to discover her own passions—there are already unhealthy expectations on her which are completely beyond her parents' control. This is an example of someone or some people objectifying a child for their own financial gain. Imagine having someone placing bets on how your child will turn out!!

3. Remove the Barriers You Have to Unconditional Love
This is probably the most important thing you can do and will fundamentally change you in positive ways. You'll be calmer, less easily annoyed, and much more loving. Your hot buttons will be turned off so it will be far more difficult to disturb your peace. This is not a quick fix and requires vigilance with your thoughts, but the results will be worth it! The method is coming up in the next chapter!

We all grow up as depleted versions of ourselves. We attempt to establish our worth out there, digging for treasure we can never find, instead of knowing that our true Worth is inside—it's Inherent. The result for far too many is addiction, bullying, depression, or eating disorders. There have been too many suicides, too many trapped in addictions or dealing with mental health disorders. That is why my goal is to help you to recognize and own your Inherent Worth, so that you can love your children unconditionally and thereby help them to grow up knowing their Inherent Worth.

KEY TAKEAWAYS

Unconditional love is rare—we all have barriers to it, and these developed when we were very young.

Unconditional love is an important factor in the mental health of your children.

- ❖ Commit to learning to love yourself to love your children unconditionally.
- ❖ Tackle the underlying causes of unwanted behavior in yourself and in your child by finding and fixing the belief that drives it.

We can't prevent our children from picking up negative beliefs as they grow up, but we can help them to shed them when they do.

The next chapter will describe a technique that can be used to heal the negative beliefs that you and your children have, and the result will be a more loving, harmonious family life and fewer problems as your children grow up.

Chapter Five

How to Turn Off Your Hot Buttons: Removing Your Barriers to Love

"If you believe you can harm then believe you can heal."
—Nachman of Bratslav

As explained in Chapter Four, the negative beliefs that all of us pick up in early childhood act as barriers to love, but they also drive our negative behaviors, such as anger, depressive thinking, frustration, impatience, and many others. By removing our barriers to love, we are simultaneously disabling our buttons and becoming a lot happier—yay! So roll up your sleeves and get ready!

Our children and our partners have a tendency to push our buttons—that's their job! It's a way of getting us to heal our negative beliefs if we let it be. We probably chose our partner because they have similar beliefs and so reflect ourselves back to us, and we get triggered at that recognition. Do you know what your buttons are? There are generally a few things that send us off the deep end or at least get us flustered. Now that you know my stories you wouldn't be surprised to learn that two of my buttons are:

1. Being embarrassed in any way. If my husband says something tactless, or if my kids did things that would bring any undue attention to me, I would get excruciatingly embarrassed. This goes back to those pirates—my belief that I'm stupid!
2. Feeling ignored or invisible. If people are not listening to what I have to say, it can be like a red flag to a bull, and yelling is the likely consequence. That goes back to the memory of my mom chopping onions instead of paying attention to me—my belief that I am worthless or inadequate.

Fortunately, I have worked to heal those beliefs to some extent and they have much less effect on me these days.

When we are angry or upset, it is because feelings or emotions have been stirred in us, and these feelings or emotions are not new—we've felt them before. In fact, the feelings we feel most often are the ones we are actually *addicted* to.

The trick to disabling your buttons is to undo the negative beliefs that you have developed over the course of your life.

These beliefs took hold of your mind in early childhood and have been strengthened since with every piece of fresh evidence you find that they are true. Of course, these beliefs are never true—you made them up when you were too young to understand the world around you. You made them up during your egocentric stage when you interpreted the events that happened around you as being your fault.

Your negative beliefs act as buttons that are easily pushed, because reactivating a negative belief takes you right back to the time that the belief was generated, and this was undoubtedly an uncomfortable situation for you. That same discomfort comes rushing right back when a triggering situation brings you the same feeling that you felt at that earlier time. An example would be when a child is rude to you and you feel a sense of anger and frustration. Those feelings of anger and frustration are the same as those that were first felt when perhaps an adult scolded you, and you made up a negative belief about yourself. It's the underlying *belief* that upsets you, not the triggering event.

This is very significant because it shifts the blame away from the child—it was not your child's fault that you became upset, the upset was about you. That's Step Two of the Six-Step Process (coming up in the next section). You have to take 100 percent responsibility for your feelings—no one else is responsible for them. So, you may *think* you're angry with your child, but that anger is really a result of a belief about *yourself* that has been triggered. It is a replay of an early incident in which anger was prominent. If you want to stop being angry with your child for not listening (or any other behavior you don't like), then you must transform the underlying belief that *chose* the anger. The Choose Again Six-Step Process is designed to do just that.

The Choose Again Six-Step Process

The Choose Again Six-Step Process (Diederik Wolsak, 2018) is used to process any current upset—any feeling of discomfort. The method is applied to any upset, however small, because these upsets reveal to us the feelings that we replay the most. These feelings are chosen by our beliefs (Fig. 1). By following our familiar feelings, we can retrieve early childhood memories in which we can discover the genesis of our beliefs and we can begin to transform them. You have to be *in the feeling* for it to work—it is a process that has to be *felt*, not an intellectual exercise. When you apply the following six steps to that upset, you will find and fix the negative belief that was triggered by the current incident.

Step 1: I'm upset. Acknowledge that you are upset. An upset can be defined as any feeling other than joy, love, or peace. It could be a slight irritation or a volcanic rage. An example would be that I'm yelling because my children aren't listening and I have something important to say to them. I'm clearly upset.

Step 2: Me. It's about Me. In this step, you take full responsibility for the way you feel in any situation. It is not your children's fault that you're upset but a negative belief that you made up in early childhood has been triggered. That your children are not listening is a completely neutral fact—it is the emotion that you are bringing to the situation that you are experiencing and that comes from an early memory. In practice, this is very difficult because we have been raised in a culture of blame. We want to blame someone else for upsetting us. We want to blame our children for making us angry. To disable your buttons, it is crucial that you understand this step—it is by far the most difficult and is resisted by most people. In my example, I have to acknowledge that my anger and frustration have *not* been caused by my children not listening but by my reaction to the situation, which is the result of an early incident in my life. Now it is my job to find out what that was.

Step 3: Focus on the feeling. Note how you feel and how strong the feeling is on a scale of 1-10. Any feeling you have or your child has is a signal that a belief is being triggered—you have work to do to find and heal it. What is the specific feeling? Use a feelings chart (Appendix C) which lists numerous different emotions to help you isolate the feelings. List them all—there are likely several—then choose the biggest two or three to process. It is likely that these are feelings that recur with some frequency in your life. Anger and frustration are the two that, in combination, led me to yell when my children weren't listening to me.

Step 4: Remember the feeling. Our feelings are closely linked to memories so ask yourself, "Is this feeling familiar?" The answer will always be "Yes," because it is linked to a negative belief that you have, which in turn is linked to a memory. So, in my example, I had the same feelings of anger and frustration when I was little in the kitchen trying to get my mom's attention to show her something, but either she couldn't hear me, or she ignored me. It is this memory of the feelings I had when I was three years old that is replaying in the present upset.

Step 5: Establish what the judgment was in the memory you retrieved in Step 4. How did you judge yourself? What did it say about you that you were treated in that way? How do you think you were judged in that situation? Our self-judgments become our core beliefs. In my example, I made up that I'm not worth being listened to. I must be worthless or my mother would hear me and be interested in what I have to show her.

Step 6: Embrace the truth of who you are. You are Inherently Worthy so you cannot be essentially flawed. Those ideas are incompatible. This step seeks to fix your mistaken belief by a process of forgiveness that replaces your mistaken belief with the truth of you—that you are Inherently Worthy, whole, and complete. This process is designed to be done by yourself. Using a mirror can be helpful. Say the recommended forgiveness formula out loud, or to yourself as follows:

"**Forgive me for believing that I'm worthless** (or whatever the mistaken belief—bad, guilty, weak, powerless, flawed, separate, etc.)." The response is, "Thank goodness that's not true! It is impossible to be worthless—you are Inherently Worthy!"

This is followed by a correction—a statement of the truth of you:

"**Forgive me for forgetting that my worth is inherent**" (or "that I am whole and complete," "love," "part of Oneness," "as the Universe intended me to be," etc.). The response is, "Thank goodness that *is* true! Your worth is a done deal—it's Inherent! It always has been and it always will be."

Use whichever words you feel comfortable using but which express your truth as an Inherently Worthy being.

If your partner is also learning this technique, then it will be very helpful to make eye contact and say the words to them. Your partner's eyes are just there to reflect you in this process, but working on this together is extremely powerful. You may need to do several rounds of "forgivenesses" for the original upset to dissipate. At this point, check back in with the level of your feelings. Has the intensity of the original upset diminished? Where are you on a scale of 1-10? If there is any residual feeling, you may need to repeat the process—perhaps a different belief has been triggered.

Go back into the early childhood memory and check the level of your feelings in that memory. Ideally, you should be able to bring that down to near zero. At this point you can explore that memory and reinterpret what was happening in a much more palatable way. In my case, I could see that my mother was busy making dinner, I can also now understand that she was almost completely deaf at that time in my life, so she didn't mean to ignore me at all. Whatever was happening in that memory said nothing about me—whatever was happening in the memory you retrieved said nothing about you. Even if a parent was shouting at you, hitting you, or being abusive, those actions said nothing about you—they were the result of the beliefs that the adult had about themselves. In this way, you can begin to undo the harm that you perceived had been done to you and disrupt the cycle.

You may well be thinking, "This is really weird!" I know I did when I was first introduced to the Six Steps in Diederik's office years ago. The fact is, it works! By stating out loud (or to ourselves) that we made a mistake in believing negative ideas about ourselves, we begin to change the old thought patterns (neural pathways) and cultivate healthier ones. It is helpful to have a formulaic way of doing this. We have to repeat this over and over again to strengthen the new pathways or the old thought patterns will begin to reassert themselves.

I wouldn't expect you to be able to use this process flawlessly on your own now. It is usually taught over a weekend or longer workshop and even then, usually needs some support on a regular basis to keep on target, but persevere and you'll be amply rewarded. Be assured that even though this seems onerous initially—it can take a while to figure out where that feeling came from—it is worth it to set some time aside at the end of the day to go over whatever upsets you may have had during the day. Eventually you'll be able to process upsets as they happen by immediately knowing what the triggering belief is and dismissing it as a false belief, and that can take just a few seconds. If every parent could recognize their triggers instantly and move from anger to love in the few seconds it takes to process the upset, just imagine how healthy, happy, resilient, and fortunate the next generation would be!

This process is radical, profound, and life-changing. It can be difficult to maintain on your own but will pay dividends if you do. See the *Resources* section (Appendix A) for details of Choose Again workshops and courses that can help you to stay on track.

From Negative Beliefs to Positive Outcomes

What you will quickly come to realize is that by doing this process many times a day, you actually begin to rewire your brain and create healthier neural pathways that lead you to a happier, lighter experience in life. You will find negative beliefs that you didn't know you had and will see how they have created patterns of behavior in your life that you wished to change. You will notice that your relationships improve—all of them, with family members, friends, coworkers, and shopkeepers. By removing barriers, you're learning to love yourself, and others—defeating the self-loathing that may well have taken hold at a subconscious level. Depression may lift, and addictions can be overcome using this method rigorously. When you see how effective it is you'll be able to help your children to see which of their negative beliefs are holding them back from a more peaceful, loving experience.

Banishing Blame

The second step, "It's about me," of the six-step process banishes blame. It states that whatever the upset, *whatever the upset*, it is about me and not about the thing I think I'm upset about. So, if your daughter has left her dishes unwashed in the sink, or your son has left his clothes lying on his bedroom floor for weeks, you must avoid the temptation of saying or thinking, "I'm upset because of the dishes or my daughter's laziness" or "I'm upset because of the clothes or that my son is sloppy." No—you are upset because at some time in your early childhood someone treated you in a way you interpreted as disrespectful, and it is the belief you made up around that idea that must be challenged. Always stop yourself from explaining why you are upset—you're likely blaming the situation or the person for your upset, but the upset is always, *always* about you! That doesn't give you permission to blame yourself either. You are not to blame. Banish expressions that begin with "because..." or "yes, but..." as this will lead you back into blaming yourself and others. Something happened to you and you are repeating over and over again your interpretation of that incident by generating the same feelings from that initiating incident and projecting them onto the current situation. It is not your fault that you chose the belief when you were too young to understand what was really happening. Being upset by your triggers is inevitable and will continue until you heal that belief, which you do by reclaiming your status as Inherently Worthy, whole, and complete.

I noticed through doing this work that I was always quick to blame others for any situation that was not to my liking. Naturally, this was not a good way to parent. I'm happy to report that, as a result of doing this work, that it is no longer the case. Being a blamer is a way of projecting responsibility onto someone else to avoid being seen in a poor light, because in some way it must have been dangerous physically or mentally to me to be "wrong." It is interesting to note the difference that taking responsibility has made in my life. It's a much more joyful experience.

Misbehavior is an opportunity for growth

Now that you see how the Six-Step Process works by using upsets to enable healing of early wounds, you'll see how what is generally deemed to be misbehavior can now be welcomed as providing a healing opportunity! Actually, with parents and children, there are healing opportunities for both parties.

When Barbara Coloroso (*Kids are Worth It!*) was a schoolteacher she had an "Opportunity Room" for children who were misbehaving. It was a place that they went, not as a punishment, but to do some problem-solving around the issue that they were having trouble with. It was an opportunity for them to grow in self-reliance and responsibility with the help of an adult who had their best interests at heart.

Similarly, you'll be a better parent when you can consider your child's misbehavior as an opportunity for growth and healing, rather than recoiling with horror that your precious child is no longer a perfect angel. If you are upset for any reason, then the Six-Step Process applies so that you can find and heal the belief that was triggered. The reason for the child's misbehavior can then be explored with a neutral, calm, problem-solving attitude.

Your child's behavior is driven by his beliefs, so checking in with his feelings will be helpful in figuring this out. Helping a child to name their feelings is always a good thing to do because being able to articulate and identify a range of feelings will allow him to heal the underlying beliefs. It will help him to get past the unpleasant feelings and calm down, and he will be able to make better choices about the feelings he wants to experience in the future.

Deescalating conflict

Any conflict can be defined as an upset, and so using the Six-Step Process will be the natural "go-to" solution. Applying the Six Steps to any conflict will result in calm for you, the parent, and for your partner or child, because they are not getting the reaction that they expect to get and which would fuel the conflict. By definition, the Six-Step Process is a conflict resolution tool.

Let's look at a specific example of a bedtime routine gone awry. Let's say that little Sammy won't go to bed and his mom is angry and frustrated because it is the third time this week. Sammy's mom thinks she is angry because of Sammy, but she is actually angry because a negative belief of hers has been triggered. She believes that she is a bad parent and therefore needs Sammy to behave well to establish her worth as a good parent. Sammy doesn't comply, so her belief that she is a bad parent is strengthened. This cycle is shown in the diagram below.

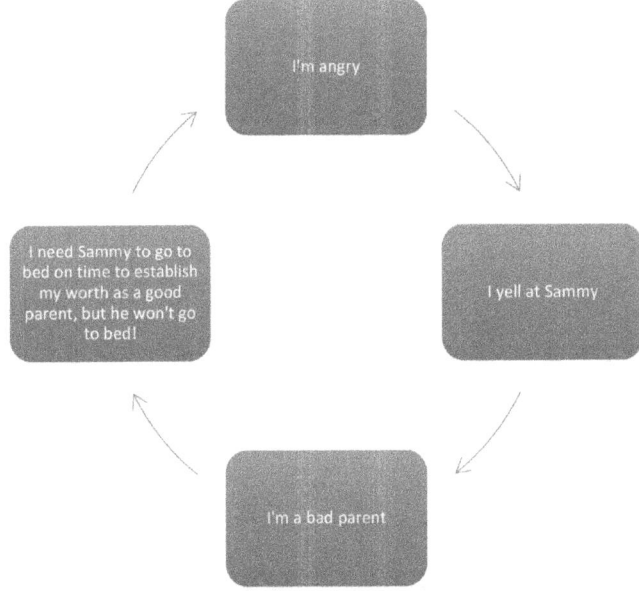

Figure 2. Parent's Belief Cycle.

Sammy has a belief that he is bad, so he will generate evidence for it by not going to bed on time. The angry response from his mom confirms his belief. When Sammy's mom processes her belief that she is a bad parent and reminds herself of her Inherent Worth, her anger subsides. Sammy no longer gets evidence from his mom that he is bad. Instead, they have a conversation about how he feels when he goes to bed late, how it feels when someone is angry with him, and how it feels when he cooperates with his parents. He can then choose to feel a whole lot better. His mom can help him to own his Inherent Worth by seeing beyond his behavior, being supportive and nonjudgmental, which is automatic when her beliefs are not being triggered. Bedtime is then the neutral fact that it is and Sammy refusing to go to bed becomes simply a problem to solve together.

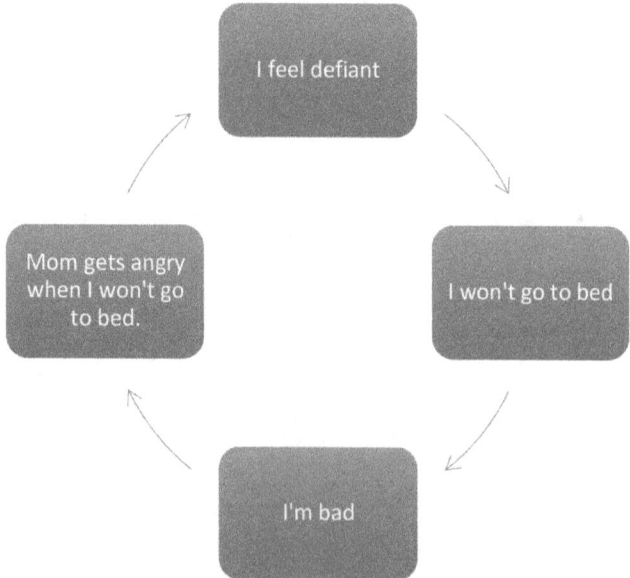

Figure 3. Sammy's Belief Cycle.

Holding the Space

Once you have used the Six-Step Process to regain your calm, no matter what is going on around you, you will be better able to do something called "holding the space" (Heather Plett, DailyGood.org). What this means is that the person who is well-trained in understanding his or her Inherent Worth (that is, the parent) will be able to see the Inherent Worth of their child and thereby allow the child to move into that space or that role. It is a way of signaling recognition nonverbally or energetically, and being sure that the person or child, who may well be acting out, will come around eventually. Never lose sight of the Inherent Worth and essential love of your children no matter how out of control they are.

KEY TAKEAWAYS

The Choose Again Six-Step Process is a powerful tool for you because it can calm you under any circumstances, while helping you to remove your barriers to love, which is essential to be able to love unconditionally.

- ❖ Use the Choose Again Six-Step Process to regain calm whenever you are "triggered."
- ❖ Identify your "hot buttons." See if you can link each to an early childhood memory.
- ❖ Understand that blame serves no one.
- ❖ Welcome misbehavior as an opportunity for growth and healing! This change in perspective makes a world of difference to all your relationships at home and at work.

Feelings are the keys to understanding the underlying beliefs that are driving behaviors—yours and your child's.

- ❖ Use age-appropriate feelings charts to help identify your own and your child's feelings.

Chapter Six

Happy Parents, Happy Kids

"The best predictor of a child's well-being is a parent's self-understanding"
–Dan Siegel, MD

As parents, we know that we teach best by example, and so the most important thing that we can do for our children is to know ourselves well and practice what we preach. It is, therefore, incumbent upon us to pay attention to our own happiness. This is not a luxury, but a necessity. That doesn't mean that you have to spend a lot of time away from your children, but it does mean noticing your emotions and doing something about them. The following section will give some specific guidelines on how to uncover the negative beliefs that are robbing you, and your child, of happiness, and will help you to regain that happiness. Here are a number of suggestions of ways you can help your children and yourself to be the happiest versions of yourselves.

1) Use the Six-Step Process when you are upset with your child.

This takes the emotion out of the reaction. Now you can deal with the problem (broken window, forgotten homework, lateness) as a neutral event and be in full problem-solving mode. Misbehavior then becomes an opportunity for growth. Your children can be involved in solving the problem and that will give them useful practical experience and build resiliency.

There may be numerous upsets within a single incident and each will need to be processed separately. Let's say your toddler just pulled a vase off the shelf at his grandparents' house and it smashed into pieces. You may react with anger and *think* you are upset with the toddler for not being careful, your parents for leaving the vase within reach, and/or yourself for not being more vigilant and watching what was going on. You or your parents may have an attachment to the vase—another upset—and the clean-up operation could supply a few more. Perhaps the vacuum cleaner isn't working or the shards of glass present a problem for the dog. Applying the Six-Step Process to each of these upsets (that is, your *feelings* about each one) results in healing underlying beliefs—a veritable gold mine! Just don't neglect Step 2—none of these upsets is about the broken vase, the child, nor the vacuum cleaner. They are all the result of triggered, mistaken, negative beliefs about who you think you are.

When a child is acting out by hitting a sibling or having a tantrum, you may well be upset. This upset can be looked at using the Six-Step Process at the time it occurs (if you are well practiced) or later if you are still finding it takes time. It is less obvious that you may be upset by a statement from a child such as, "Mommy—I'm bored!"

Of course, this may not even create a ripple of a reaction in anyone who doesn't have a belief that is triggered by it, but let's assume for this example, that you do react to it:

"Mommy, I'm bored!"

There's a good chance that hearing these words will trigger us in some way. Perhaps we'll feel guilty. "Oh no, I'm not a good parent—otherwise my child wouldn't be bored. I haven't provided enough activities or encouraged enough independence for them to find something to do on their own!"

Job number one, then, is to process your own upset over the statement. It's about **me** that I feel upset—not about my child feeling bored. If you sit with that feeling of guilt for a few minutes you'll remember a time when you felt guilty as a child. Whatever you did that you perceived to be wrong at that time was something you did because of a belief that you were bad, and it is time to forgive yourself for that belief. You can remind yourself that it is not possible to taint your innermost, Inherently Worthy, true self in any way. If you can remind yourself to reconnect with that pure part of yourself, you will no longer feel guilty.

Eventually, that process can be done in the few seconds it takes to recognize that your child's statement caused a reaction—an upset—in you.

Now, it is just a neutral fact that your child expressed boredom. Now you can tackle that as a problem to be solved.

So, what did your child actually mean when she said she was bored?

Here are a few possibilities:

- I need entertaining to be happy
- I need your attention to be happy
- I'm not being directed—help!
- Things are not OK as they are—something needs to be different
- There is an emptiness that must be filled
- Help! I'm not comfortable with my thoughts and need to be distracted from them.

If we comply by helping our children to fill their time with activities that we suggest, we will not be helping them to cope with being alone with their own selves, and their own thoughts. We'll be helping them to avoid the real issue, which is a mistaken belief they hold about needing something external for them to be happy.

So, express confidence in their ability to find something interesting to do or encourage them to delight in not being busy—time for meditation, reading, or just "being." Unstructured playtime is considered to be essential for children to develop life skills (Dr. Shimi Kang, *The Dolphin Parent*). Beware of filling every waking moment with activity. Children need more down time.

If you have a gratitude habit (and if not then be sure to institute one), a useful thing you could do is express your own gratitude for the ordinary wonderful things in life: a conversation you had with someone that taught you something you didn't already know, something unusual you saw in the garden, something you read in a book, a sentence that caused you to see things differently, or some words that just sounded great together. These examples will help to show your children how much richness there is all around us. There is no reason to ever be bored!

Nachman of Bratslav said: "*Seek the sacred within the ordinary. Seek the remarkable within the commonplace.*" Helping our children to do this by doing this ourselves will go a long way to solving boredom.

This is just one example of a possible trigger statement, but think about others that might cause a reaction in you. How about, "I hate you!" (a rite of passage for many parents), "You're mean!" or "You stink!" It takes a well-trained parent not to have an unpleasant gut reaction to any of these and many other statements. Stay the course and adopt the mindset that "this is for my healing" and engage the Six-Step Process to regain your equanimity.

A NOTE ABOUT SCREEN TIME

One of the biggest causes of upsets for parents currently seems to be the battle over screen time. Studies show that too much screen time is not good for children, and screens need to be off for an hour or two before bedtime or sleep can suffer. Policing screen time is an unwelcome but necessary chore for parents these days.

When my children were still in elementary school I became so frustrated at the incessant watching of

TV, and my inability to do anything about it, that I took the TV and placed it on the sidewalk for anyone to take away. My children remember that with horror to this day and I am not particularly proud of it—it was just a demonstration of my being upset because my mistaken belief that "I am a failure" was triggered. Had I been armed at that time with the Choose Again Six-Step Process, I would simply have processed my upset and then dealt with screen time calmly as a problem to be solved. My equanimity would have guaranteed that the kids would have been willing to participate in a conversation about alternatives to TV, reasons why it needs to be limited, and priority-setting—how to decide which programs to watch and which to abandon.

Those were the good old days when screen time only involved TV and video games. Now, with cell phones and laptops, Snapchat and Instagram, screen time is a whole lot more complicated, infinitely more accessible, and much more of a minefield for parents and children. Still, the basic approach will be the same:

First, process your own upsets around use or misuse of screen time by you and your children. Remember that this is not about screen time, it's about you. It is highly likely that the underlying belief is, "I'm not good enough," "I'm a bad parent," or "I'm useless, worthless, or inadequate." From a neutral, emotion-free standpoint, it will be easier to set limits and be firm in applying rules around screen time.

Next, find out why your child *thinks* he is engaging in screen time. A few possibilities:

- The need to vegetate because of too many demands at school or home
- Peer pressure
- Addiction to the stimulation of video games
- Fear of social isolation if they don't engage in social media posts
- Fear of not being "in the know" with TV shows, movies, or games

Each of these "reasons" has a negative belief beneath it. Time to do a little digging…The way to find these is to ask about the feelings that he has about screen time. How would it feel if he wasn't up to date on the latest shows? How would he feel if he didn't advance to the next level in his latest game? What is the feeling he gets when his phone has to go into a box during mealtimes and homework hour? How does it feel when there are demands on his time at home and school?

Helping him to process his feelings will be useful in trying to help your child reduce or limit screen time. The underlying beliefs that screen time covers up are likely some combination of "I'm alone," "I'm not good enough," "I don't belong," and "I'm not worthy." Reminding him that these are not true

> and that his Worth is Inherent will go a long way to easing any changes that need to be made.
>
> If you have raised your children to know their Inherent Worth, and to have a sense of purpose, they will be less likely to fill their available time with screen time. Leading by example will be the best way to help children to deal with the pressures of the screens in their lives. Be sure to have screen-free family activities such as neighborhood walks, board games, chores that are done together, and opportunities for giving back to the community as a family. Having a sense of purpose and positive connections with family and friends will work as an antidote to the excessive need for screen time.
>
> In many families, screen time is a useful babysitter. Be gentle with yourself if this is your reality. Gradually over time as you move from fear-based parenting to love-based parenting, you will find yourself more relaxed and increasingly able to find time to share fun activities with your child that don't involve screens. It can be very helpful to set this as a goal.

2) Guilt has got to go!

Innocence-maintenance is a job we can help our children with, so be your child's guilt-buster! If your child does something wrong, make sure that guilt is not an ongoing problem. Self-loathing starts early, so it needs to be tackled early. In fact, suicide prevention and addiction prevention begin in preschool (and younger) by tackling the guilt and other negative beliefs children pick up as they grow.

Never use guilt as a management tool nor remind them of how guilty they are. Even when we don't consciously do this, guilt has a way of being transmitted from parents to children. I recently saw a cartoon which pictured a mother sitting in a café with her adult daughter. Her daughter says to her, "I feel I need you less, now that I can make myself feel guilty on my own!" Guilt has to go. Remind children that they are not guilty when they make mistakes. Mistakes are inevitable as we grow up and we can learn from them. They don't change the essence of who we are. As you know by now, children give themselves life sentences in the form of a negative belief that they are guilty for small misdeeds, and you are likely still enslaved by some of yours!

Several years ago, I asked a group of fourth grade students if they could describe what guilt feels like. They could. They described it as "gut-wrenching" and "excruciating"! What could children in fourth grade possibly have done in their lives that could justify them carrying guilt around? At that age? We all have unhealthy doses of guilt, but why? We all have trouble forgiving ourselves when we do something wrong. Many of us are still serving out the life sentences we gave ourselves as children, but the Six-Step Process can free you!

Your job as a parent is to limit how much your children punish themselves by helping them to shed their guilt. This is a challenging concept for many, because, yes—you did those things or your child did those things and are guilty as charged. The Six-Step Process does not condone bad behavior. Whatever the guilty behavior caused is a neutral fact and a problem to be solved when calm minds can tackle it. The point is that the truth of who you are and who your child is has never changed, and being in touch with the reality of your Inherent Worth will ensure that there are fewer and fewer guilty incidents moving forward, when the belief "I'm guilty" is reduced or healed. This is actually a reversal of cause and effect.

MARCUS

When I was co-facilitating the workshop *Finding Meaning in Life* at a retreat center in the South of France we had a fifty-five-year-old participant with advanced terminal cancer, in search of peace. Most of Marcus's processes (using the Six Steps) in the days before he died were to release the idea he had that he was "F***ing bad news!" His mother had often told him that he was a nail in her coffin and that if he'd been born first (he was the youngest of six) he would have been an only child.

The day before he died he came to the circle having had a bad night in which lots of fear had come up. He told us that he didn't fear dying, nor getting well again, but he feared staying in the same condition for a long time, which he felt was a burden to others. We explored the fear that he was feeling (knowing that this was not about being a burden, but about

Marcus) and it revealed an early childhood memory in which he had found himself in his pajamas outside his home in the middle of the night. He had been sleepwalking and had no idea how he got there. The door was locked and he couldn't make enough noise to rouse his brothers. His commotion did, however, wake the neighbors and they helped him get back in.

A little probing revealed that the fear he experienced as that little boy was about the punishment that he expected to get as a result of his predicament, rather than about being outside in the dark alone. Even though punishment for Marcus was frequent and painful, it said nothing about him. It merely indicated the pain his parents were in at the time. The forgiveness that Marcus did in the circle was for having innocently and mistakenly chosen to believe that he was the epitome of evil and that he deserved to be punished. That seemed to give him a visible sense of relief. He understood that it was finally time to stop punishing *himself.* The last words he said in the circle were, "I am innocent," which he said with conviction to everyone in the circle individually. Marcus died peacefully in his sleep that night on the last day of the workshop.

I tell Marcus's story to illustrate that our negative beliefs are life sentences that we give ourselves. We don't want our children to carry their guilt and other negative beliefs around with them year after year, so we must challenge them at every opportunity.

3) Help children clue into their feelings.

It is important to allow children to feel their feelings and express their emotions. If they are not allowed to do so, they will internalize their distress and create evidence for their negative beliefs. Home should be a safe place for children to experience their feelings. Your job is to help them to label and recognize the feelings that they are having and as they get older, help them use their emotions as indicators of their mistaken beliefs. Use feelings charts to help them identify their feelings—there are several that you can find online that are designed for kids. Young children can use pictures of facial expressions that illustrate feelings and point to the ones they are feeling.

Help your child to recognize the feelings that she is having in different situations so that she can decide which situations feel better than others and make choices based on how she wants to feel. By that I mean, ask your child how she's feeling when she is contentedly reading a book, or doodling on a piece of paper, or helping bake cookies, and at other times when she might not be so content, such as when she's just lost a game that she was playing with a friend, or when a house of cards fell down.

And of course, it is important to ask about feelings around misbehavior: Ask, "How did you feel when you stepped on your brother's toe and he started to cry?" rather than "Why did you step on your brother's toe?" which is an accusation. Ask, "How would it feel to have a tidy room?" rather than "Why haven't you tidied your room? I reminded you yesterday!" Kids may believe that they don't deserve to feel good. A parent's reaction to a messy room is what the child is looking for, so helping her to be aware of her Inherent Worth may actually lead to a tidier room and a happier child.

4) Find the root cause of a child's behavior.
You also now know that behavior is driven by a negative belief that your child has developed. That's helpful. You know that you need to find the **root cause**. You can probably guess at the belief beneath it and maybe even why they have developed that belief.

Here are a few examples:

- **Bullying** behavior can result from a child believing he's weak and powerless, bad, guilty, or unlovable.
- Being picked on as a **victim** can also result from an underlying belief in weakness—that vibe can be picked up by a bully resulting in a bully/victim relationship, in which they both share the same underlying belief. It is helpful if the bully and the victim can process together to heal their respective beliefs. I have included my blog about raising bully-proof children in Appendix D.
- **Anxiety** can result from any number of beliefs, including, "I'm not safe" or "I'm not lovable" or "I can lose love."
- **Depression** can result from "I'm not loved" or "I'm not good enough" or "I'm worthless." Any of the negative beliefs can result in depression, because they act as barriers to love, and depression can be seen as a feeling of a lack of love. This is why depression responds so readily to the Choose Again Six-Step Process, which finds and heals these barriers, allowing love in.
- **Perfectionism** is usually a result of a child feeling worthless. They try to establish worth by how well they do things.

If your child expresses any of these beliefs as negative self-criticism, the appropriate response is, "Is it true that you are...?" "No, it's not! You are whole and complete, there's nothing wrong with you." Remind them, "Your worth is a done deal. It is not established by...(whatever the child believes he lacks)." Use any or all of the strategies given in Chapter Three to counter these beliefs.

THE PERILS OF PERFECTIONISM

My daughter was a perfectionist in her last couple of years of elementary school and into eighth grade in high school. Her behavior got more and more extreme until she would rip up a whole page of homework because the last word was slightly wonky or a word misspelled. It was agonizing watching her beat herself up over any perceived imperfection, yet the imperfections were inevitable—it just isn't possible to be completely perfect. There is always another level of perfection to aspire to. We tried to help her to see that "good enough" was good enough, but it didn't work.

Perfectionism is a trait that is common in girls (and boys) with eating disorders (*Psychology Today*). They may strive for the perfect body to prove their worth when the underlying belief is one of worthlessness. Some of these girls and boys would prove to be anything but perfect in the years following their eating disorders. Disordered eating is just the first step in what for many was a gradual progression to more and

> more self-destructive behaviors. Perfectionism has been found to be a predictive factor in suicide ideation according to Paul Hewitt et al. (*Journal of Abnormal Child Psychology*, 1997). For our daughter it progressed to drinking, smoking, and other forms of self-loathing.
>
> Perfectionism is a big red flag, so please don't ignore it. It can lead to heartache and heartbreak if left unchallenged. The antidote is not simply trying to show that good enough is good enough, or counseling to set more realistic goals—these are attempts to change the symptom—but there is a real need to counter the negative beliefs that drive it. The antidote to negative beliefs is the concept that everyone has Inherent Worth. Our worth is not established by how neatly we do our homework, nor by getting 100 percent on a test. Our worth is inherent—we need do nothing to earn it. This thought may cause concern to parents and teachers who believe that children won't try hard if they are told this, and who don't want to interfere with the "success" that a child appears to be having because of their perfectionist tendencies, but it could save a child's life. In the long term, a child will be much more successful and resilient if the negative beliefs that drive perfection are challenged and replaced with the certain understanding that he or she has IW.

Just remember that even if you don't know what the triggering belief is, the antidote is *always* to help with awareness of Inherent Worth. Strategies for this were given in Chapter Three.

5) Beware of giving a hidden message that directly feeds a belief.

The nonverbal messages that we transmit to each other and to our children are just as capable of feeding negative beliefs as the verbal ones. A gesture as small as an eyebrow lifting or a roll of the eyes can give a child the message that they are far less important than whatever it is I am doing at the time, and that their concerns are trivial. The beliefs "I'm not important" or "I don't matter" will be fed and strengthened as a result.

Have you ever withheld information from a parent because you thought that it would be better for them (or for you) if they didn't know? Perhaps your elderly parents or grandparents would worry if you told them you were going to the doctor, so you elect not to mention it. You want to protect your parents from worrying unnecessarily because you know there is nothing they can do about it in any case. It's the same with children—they don't want you to worry about them. If you get worried about something they have done or will do, you are inadvertently giving them the message that they are not safe, not capable, and that they are vulnerable. These are messages that directly feed negative beliefs which many children will develop by the time they are eight years old: "I'm weak and powerless," "I'm not capable," "I'm not safe." As parents, we tend to feed our child's beliefs without knowing that we are doing it.

What's the message we transmit when we help our children with their homework? That they are not capable enough without our help and that grades are of supreme importance. Of course, it is often the loving thing to do to assist a child in understanding new material or making a connection with it to their lives, but if we constantly feel that we have to nag our children to get their homework done, and if it matters to us what grade they get, then we are feeding them unhealthy ideas.

What's the message we give when we tidy their room for them, rather than letting them do it themselves? This tells them that they are not capable of doing a good enough job unless I do it for them. It also could inadvertently give a subconscious message that they don't belong—this is my house not theirs and I need it to look a certain way.

What's the message we give if we come home from work exhausted and grumpy, complaining about our day? Our children will deduce that "life is hard," "it's a joyless world," and that there is really nothing to look forward to when they grow up.

My father used to come home from a day in the operating room and read his newspaper. He probably needed this as a transition from a stressful working environment, but for me his newspaper acted as an impenetrable barrier between us. I was shut out from his life and in my mind, also his love.

What's the message we give our children if we make sacrifices so that they can have more opportunities? This is a trick question because the word "sacrifice" is charged. Sacrifice implies that the thing being given is lost to the one doing the giving. It is associated with a sense of "lack"—a sense that there is a finite amount of love and therefore not enough to go around.

My father sacrificed a promotion for him to move our family to a town where my brother and I would get a better education. Had he done this purely out of love, it would have been fine, but there was a lingering element of regret for him personally, because he never received the promotion that he would have had, and so the unspoken message we received was that we owed him our good grades and our achievements, otherwise his sacrifice would not have been worthwhile. Had he instead just decided that this was the loving thing to do and never looked back, this would not have been a "sacrifice" for him, and we would have been free to achieve or not, and would have had less pressure and greater happiness as a result. We would have had a closer relationship with our father as well.

What's the message we give our children when we sign them up for extracurricular activities because we think a new skill would look good on a college application form, even though they are busy already? We are telling them that they are not good enough as they are, that they need to be shaped to become more musical, a better athlete, or more conversant in another language. They may also wonder whose life this is anyway. Despondency can result from the feeling of having every area of their lives controlled by a parent. Sometimes a parent will encourage a child who shows an aptitude, but then take over by getting too excited and too involved. Putting art on public display, starting a business selling something the child has made, or having them perform for their grandmother's friends may actually *discoura*ge a child. That child may then decide that he no longer wants to engage in the activity that started this whole cycle in the first place.

What's the message I give you when I worry about you? You're not safe or you're not capable.

What's the message I give you when you come home with a D grade and I'm upset? You're responsible for my feelings. You're not good enough.

What's the message I give you when I get excited when you come home with an "A" on your report card? You've made me happy. You'd better keep bringing A grades. My worth depends on your "A" or your worth depends on your "A."

What's the message I give you when I praise every picture you paint no matter how messy it is? I don't really care about your picture, I just know that I'm supposed to give you lots of praise. I'm not that interested in your process or what the challenges were—just in your achievements.

What is the message I give myself when I win a competition? I shouldn't have won, now I have to win every time. I'm the best—other people are losers! Really, that means that I think I'm a loser. My worth is established by winning competitions—I'm out of luck if I don't keep winning.

What's the message I give you when I assign chores that I don't pay for? You are a valued member of the family. We are relying on you to do your part. You matter. Giving children chores, which are not paid for, is a way of helping children to understand that they are part of the family system—that others rely on them playing their part. It is a strong message of belonging and capability. The chores need to be age-appropriate, but even very young children can help out. At sixteen months old, my granddaughter loved to empty the clothes from the dryer into a basket!

Dr. Deborah Gilboa (*Get the Behavior You Want...Without Being the Parent You Hate!*) gave her children chores that helped the whole family and reports that although the kids complained to her, they actually bragged to their friends about their abilities! At seven her children would do the laundry for the whole family; at nine, make the school lunches for themselves and their siblings; at eleven, load and unload the dishwasher and tidy the kitchen; at thirteen, make dinner once a week for the family. She also notes that a study shows that children who had chores that were helpful to the family spend more of their free time hanging out with their family because they developed a strong sense of belonging.

6) Lose the labels.

Labels act a lot like negative beliefs. Children become their labels. The bad kid in a family will be the bad kid in the family, the klutz will be the klutz until freed of those labels. Children who are labeled as learning disabled may cease trying and feel that they have no hope because they have been given an excuse for low expectations.

Diederik Wolsak (2018) reports just that when he was working with high school students who were predominantly First Nations and "at-risk" kids who had experienced child abuse. He asked them what was the worst thing that ever happened to them. One girl raised her hand and told him that it was the day she was told that she had to have remedial help for her learning disabilities. She no longer had to try hard at school and gave up hope of a bright future.

There are times when it is helpful to have a diagnosis so that appropriate learning strategies can be put into place for a child at school. It would be wonderful if parents, teachers, and principals would help children to understand everyone learns in a different way, and it doesn't mean that anyone is better or worse than anyone else because of it. Taking the emphasis off grades and putting it onto kindness will help with this.

Labels objectify the person being labeled and so "people first" language is important to adopt when talking about someone who has been labeled. This means instead of saying "He's ADD" rather say "He's a boy with ADD." Rather than saying "She's Down Syndrome" say "She is a girl with Down Syndrome." It is a small but significant adjustment to be aware of and to teach kids. Ultimately and ideally, *all* labels will be unnecessary.

7) Demonstrate your own commitment to processing upsets.

This is particularly important when you are parenting an unhappy child but applies to parenting any child. Here are a few reasons why being a happy parent actually helps a child:

- ❖ It demonstrates to children that life is a joy—it's worth living!
- ❖ It demonstrates that parents value themselves and take care of their own mental health. This is what being a great role model is all about.
- ❖ When a parent is happy despite their child being miserable, that parent no longer adds to the burden of guilt that the child is feeling. The child can no longer drag the parent down and so can no longer reap the

evidence for guilt (a negative belief) that doing so brings.
- ❖ You have a right to be happy! No one can take your happiness away from you—only your thoughts can do that.

Perhaps the thought of doing something for yourself or even attempting to be happy when your child is on the verge of complete disaster induces guilt. You may be thinking, as I did, that it isn't possible to be happy when the child you adore is behaving in ways that you cannot fathom, but I have come to believe that it is imperative to try. For one thing, it will improve your health, mentally and physically.

Surprisingly, the years during which my daughter was battling eating disorders, smoking, and drinking were among my happiest to date. I gave myself permission to exercise, went to therapy, took time for myself, and developed all my hobbies. I had been a workaholic while my kids were growing up and we had taken very little time to have fun as a family. This may have inadvertently contributed to our daughter's problems in the first place. When we weren't working we were doing chores.

My daughter was so relieved when I finally stopped being dragged down by her—we were able to release our co-dependencies and she began to improve even before she chose to do her own work with the same therapist because of the results she had seen in me.

It may be difficult to comprehend, but I was able to reach a place of gratitude to my daughter for having the problems that she did, because it prompted me, out of necessity, to discover how to be happy, and provided a way for us to renew our strong, loving bond that had been severely tested. She gained tremendous resilience as a result of her journey as well.

Learning to love unconditionally has the added benefit of changing our own and our children's behavior by healing the beliefs that not only once acted as barriers to love, but also once prompted poor behavior that brought further evidence for these false beliefs. Applying the Six-Step Process to any and all upsets will be extremely effective in changing behavior of parents and children because it will enhance the awareness of the Inherent Worth of each.

Parenting became an opportunity for personal transformation for me and my husband. It can be that for you too.

KEY TAKEAWAYS

We all make up beliefs about ourselves based on our experiences in the world.

- ❖ Become proficient in using the Choose Again Six-Step Process to uncover your negative beliefs and begin to question and heal them.

These beliefs act as barriers to love and to knowing that we have Inherent Worth, and they drive our subsequent behavior.

- ❖ Notice shifts in your behavior as a result of frequent use of the Six-Step Process.
- ❖ Innocence-maintenance is a job we can help our children with. Guilt has to go.

Feelings are the indicators of negative beliefs in play, so it's important to help children to recognize their feelings.

- ❖ Find an age-appropriate feelings chart online or at an education store and display it at home.
- ❖ Refer to the feelings chart to help your children clue into their feelings.

In the final section, we will look at how parenting from a place of love, rather than a place of fear, makes all the difference. We'll explore how to recognize each "mode" and how to move from fear to love.

PART THREE

Parenting Priorities:
Kindness Versus Grades

Chapter Seven

Parenting with Purpose

*"The meaning of life is to find your gift.
The purpose of life is to give it away."*

–Pablo Picasso

We all lead very busy lives. There is one thing that can help us simplify a little and that is having a strong sense of purpose. Knowing your purpose gives you a framework within which to make decisions. It can inform your parenting in a profound way. It helps keep you focused and avoid distractions. It provides you with a clear direction. If you know your life's purpose, you can be far more intentional in all your activities and it provides an endless source of motivation.

Have you given much thought to your purpose? It is not generally something we are encouraged to do. Without purpose, however, we are at the mercy of the media, of advertising, of entertainment, and of society to fill our empty spaces and to provide that direction for us. We blindly go along with the crowd. There is a remarkably accurate portrayal of this in a short, animated clip on YouTube by Steve Cutts, called "Happiness." It shows hordes of rats chasing happiness in all the wrong places—shopping malls, glamorous movies, money—and exposes the futility of their empty, unhappy lives. Their hurry to get where they are going (the rat race) leads to violence, dysfunction, and tremendous unhappiness. None of them stops for a moment to consider their purpose. Without purpose, we are those unhappy rats. Without a sense of purpose, teenagers (and others) may fill the void with drugs, screen time, inappropriate sexual activity, or other negative behaviors—a misguided kind of "seeking."

In this chapter, I'll present some ideas about life's purpose from a number of traditions, because it is remarkable how fundamental kindness seems to be to all of them. Of course, you don't have to subscribe to any formal religion to be kind and to have a sense of purpose! We'll also look at how kindness relates to our purpose, and the importance of kindness to our mental well-being.

Purpose

What do you think we are here for?

The biblical injunction to "Love your neighbor as yourself" seems like pretty good advice. It is central to the Torah (*Leviticus 19:18*) and to the New Testament (*Mark 12:31*), suggesting that extending love to others is of primary importance and that we need to love ourselves as well. The golden rule is another gem—"Don't do to others what you wouldn't have them do to you" (the Jewish version) or "Do unto others as you would have them do unto you" (the Christian version). It implies that acts of kindness are the way to live and to love.

The Dalai Lama, the Tibetan Buddhist leader who is widely acknowledged to be a beacon of peace and love in the world and a happy person, simply states: "My religion is kindness." It couldn't be plainer than that.

I was fortunate enough to meet a woman named Bracha Kapach, who was the embodiment of human kindness. She devoted her life to making the lives of others better by responding to their needs. She held summer camps for neighborhood children and provided dinners for numerous families every week from a freezer on her porch. She collected wedding dresses for poor brides, wedding bands for grooms, and even catered hundreds of weddings personally. Her garage was stacked from floor to ceiling with secondhand clothes and items that could be given to those in need. No wonder that miracles of various types were attributed to her over the years. She summed up life's purpose simply as "Life is doing good deeds," which she did until the day she died in her late eighties.

All these ideas involve loving and being kind to others. Diederik Wolsak, whose advice (based on his own remarkable transformation and his ability to transform others) informs much of this book, similarly teaches that our purpose is to give and receive love. In other words, to be kind. The book *A Course in Miracles* (Foundation for Inner Peace) further indicates that giving is receiving and that we receive the love that we give instantaneously, whether or not it's returned by the person to whom it's being given. This is another major healing principle that can help people to recover from addictions, eating disorders, and other negative behaviors. Asking "How can I serve?" on a daily basis is one way of ensuring that our purpose is focused on helping ourselves and others connect to our Inherent Worthiness. I have personally found it to be simple enough to use as an everyday guide yet profound enough to provide a sense of fulfillment.

None of the above purposes involves climbing high on the ladder, getting ahead of others, or being at the top academically. In fact, in the Bible, the characters favored by God had attributes of kindness. Nowhere does it say that anyone was a grade A math student or a genius at languages. Sarah and Abraham were known for their hospitality, Rebecca for her kindness to animals. Moses was a shepherd and his kindness to his sheep got him the job of leading slaves to freedom. Not bad.

Kindness is key and yet the pursuit of so-called excellence has become the path that many parents today wish their children to embark on. We need to ask ourselves what excellence is for. Why do we hold excellence so dear? Excellence is not an end in itself.

Consider that excellence and achievement are ideas that were held in high regard by Nazis in their quest to develop an efficient killing machine and establish themselves as the "master race." Athletes such as Lance Armstrong achieved greatness but took performance-enhancing drugs to get there. The Russian Olympic team was banned because of a system of cheating. The notion that using doping and other unfair advantages is alright, as long as you don't get caught, undermines the stated purpose of the games and makes a mockery of fair play. What is the price of excellence and achievement if they promote cheating and unkindness—even genocide—in their pursuit?

When we are clear about our purpose as having something to do with kindness, then everything can serve that purpose. Our job, our relationships, our parenting—all serve as vehicles for giving and receiving love. To give an everyday example in which having a sense of purpose led to greater peace and happiness, my husband recently got stuck in traffic, as often happens in Vancouver, trying to cross the Lion's Gate Bridge. He was with his dad and stepmom. Instead of being triggered by the forty-five-minute delay, he simply reminded himself of his purpose—to give and receive love—and enjoyed the time spent in the car with his parents. A quick reframe of almost any situation in this way will lead to a greater sense of calm.

It is perhaps not a surprise that *giving* is very difficult for people with mental health issues such as eating disorders or addictions, because so much of their time is taken up in the business of simply surviving. When my daughter was struggling with eating disorders and self-harming behaviors, I was fully aware of the benefits of extending kindness, so with the help of a good friend I was able to arrange for her to paint the nails of residents at a local home for elders. She went a couple of times but was unable to maintain her commitment—the good feelings she got from helping went against the powerful beliefs she had that she was bad and guilty. Establishing helping relationships when children are younger will help to head off problems before they start but may be difficult to initiate when problems are in full swing.

If our ultimate purpose is to be kind, then why are we so fixated on getting our kids into the "best" schools? Why are we loading them up with extracurricular activities? If we are clear about our sense of purpose, we can set more appropriate intentions and goals for our families and be more successful in experiencing happiness.

Kindness is Good for Us

I think we can all agree that we'd like to live in a kinder, gentler world than the one we appear to be living in at the moment. Here's the good news: Kindness is good for us.

Dr. Lara Aknin (Simon Fraser University) co-authored a study with University of British Columbia colleagues Kiley Hamlin and Elizabeth Dunn ("Giving Leads to Happiness in Young Children") which showed that toddlers under two years old displayed greater happiness in giving their own treats to another, rather than giving away extra treats that were supplied for them to give away. This study busted the myth that toddlers are selfish and showed that positive emotions are associated with giving. Another study (Elizabeth Dunn and Ashley Willans, 2015) found a link between generosity and happiness in adults.

If I do a kind deed for someone, I will get a good feeling (giving is receiving). That good feeling will help me to overcome some of my negative self-talk. If I am in the habit of doing good deeds, I will be in touch with the truth of who

I am—an Inherently Worthy being. It'll improve my awareness that I have Inherent Worth.

The point here is that being kind has very important consequences for our mental health.

When we extend love, we access our higher selves—that part of our self that is connected to everyone and everything. It has tremendous power. Encouraging children to engage in kind deeds gives them a sense of their personal power. Being kind and being generous helps us to access the happiness that exists inside each of us that we want to experience and want our children to experience.

Kindness *versus* Grades

In my role as an educator, I became a student of Danny Siegel (master educator, author and poet). I spent one summer working with him in Jerusalem, learning from him and from *his* teachers, who are his heroes. These are people who demonstrate unusual kindness and creativity in helping others. Danny brings youth groups to meet with and learn from these people. Over the course of fifty or so years that Danny has been doing this he has introduced over six thousand students to them. One of the things that Danny does and had me do too is "work the bus" on our way from place to place. During this time, he would always ask the students what is the one thing that would make your parents happy. Without fail the students said, "Good grades." *Every one of them.* Danny also does lecture tours around North America, and at these times he usually speaks to adults. He invariably asks the adults what they want for their kids. They respond that they want them to be happy, healthy, and kind. They *never* mention good grades. Why the disconnect?

Children receive the message that grades are important the first time they bring an A home and we get excited about it. I wrote about being careful with praise in Chapters Two and Three, and this is why. Remember those hidden messages I mentioned in Chapter Six? Children will always receive the underlying message even when it is not expressed verbally. They may even believe that their parents' love is conditional on getting good grades. They may believe that their worth is established by their grades.

As Danny noted, "Teenagers are swept up in the pursuit of excellence and achievement, and the sensation of competitiveness for good grades is often brutal—it takes a toll on the teenagers' well-being." Danny's essay on "Getting As and/or Being a *Mensch*" was the inspiration for the story I wrote, which was published as *The Radiance of the Lights* (Appendix E), which I'll summarize here:

A Tale of Two Students

The story is about an education system gone wrong and what was needed to fix it.

Jonathan represents a high-achieving student in that flawed system. Miriam, on the other hand, is a student who has had access to a different educational influence.

Both students have exactly the same program—they are both studying hard to get into medical school. They both volunteer at a home for the aged and they both play the clarinet. When the question is posed to the students, "Why do they do what they do?" their answers are very different.

Miriam is studying to get into medical school because she has heard about a village in India where there is an unusually large population of people with cleft palates. She wants to be able to help them, so she'd like to be a surgeon. She visits the home for the aged to learn from one of the volunteers there who is skilled in the art of "Gentle Human Touch." She learned to play the clarinet to have a useful skill—something that she can use to help others—either by entertaining them or raising money for the cleft palate operations.

Jonathan, on the other hand, is hoping to get into med school to please his parents. His father is a famous plastic surgeon and Jonathan needs to impress him to make him proud. He goes to the home for the aged to get his volunteer hours and needs his clarinet-playing to look good on his application.

Miriam is motivated by kindness or love. She is motivated by what she can give. Jonathan is motivated by fear—fear of not having his parents' love if he doesn't succeed. He is motivated by what he can get.

It is easy to see which of these students is under the most pressure. Miriam has a "Why?" to live by and will find another path to achieve her goal if she doesn't get into medical school. Jonathan, on the other hand, needs to get into medical school and may even be tempted to cheat to do so. How might he react if he doesn't get in? He will be at risk of falling into depression or worse.

Miriam is better equipped to handle life's ups and downs. The character Miriam in my story was based on a real student. She didn't get into medical school on her first try but took the opportunity to spend a year getting a master's degree in community health, worked with AIDS patients in Africa, and got into medical school on her second try. Jonathan, also based on a real student, did get into the university program of his choice, but cheated along the way. I haven't followed his progress, but I would not be surprised to hear he has constant stress and a poor quality of life as a result.

Kindness is a good motivator. The reason I wrote this story, other than to honor Danny Siegel, is to illustrate that kindness doesn't have to be instead of academic achievement but can enhance the motivation to do well academically.

Craig Kielburger, the CEO of "Free the Children" and "ME to WE" (multinational children's organizations that promote youth leadership), was motivated by his strong desire to end child slavery. His determined pursuit of his goal has resulted in him being the youngest person ever to receive the Order of Canada. He attended the University of Toronto, the Schulich School of Business at York University, and the Kellogg School of Management at Northwestern University, to gain the expertise that he needed to work towards his goal.

Craig is just one example of many for whom the "Why?" to do something drives the "How?" Helping our children to be curious about our world will help them to develop the "Why?" that will help guide the course of their lives.

> *"When someone has a 'Why?' to live they*
> *can cope with almost any 'How?'"*
> *–Victor Frankl*

KEY TAKEAWAYS

Having a sense of purpose in our lives helps us to keep a healthy perspective on the little things that happen in our family's day to day interactions. It helps to keep us motivated and eases decision-making.

- ❖ Discuss with your family what you stand for as a family—can you define your purpose?

Kindness trumps grades, but they are not mutually exclusive.

- ❖ Prioritize kindness.
- ❖ Ask your child about the kind acts they have done or witnessed during their day at school.

Having a sense of purpose can help teens to avoid negative behaviors such as substance abuse or self-harm and can mitigate the impact of social media and screen time.

- ❖ Talk to your teen about your own sense of purpose.
- ❖ Ask them if they have ever thought about the meaning of life or what their purpose is.

Regaining our sense of purpose will help ensure a kind future for ourselves and our children.

Chapter Eight
Strategies for Raising Kind Kids

*"When I was young I admired clever people.
Now that I am old I admire kind people."*
–Abraham Joshua Heschel

In this chapter, I'll suggest a few ways that parents can nurture kindness in themselves and in their children. There's one important point that I should mention up front, and that is that unkind people have the same Inherent Worth as those who are kind. Kindness should not be a prerequisite for someone to have before you'll extend love to them. Being loved unconditionally and growing up with awareness of Inherent Worth will, however, naturally lead to kind behavior.

Having said that, I firmly believe that there is much to be learned from experts on how to extend love to others and that knowledge may inspire children to be like them. Just be sure not to push children into doing kind deeds that they are not into, or not ready for. Children know when we are manipulating them, and this is no exception. They will detect when Mom or Dad is trying to get them to do something nice to improve behavior, change an attitude, or make them proud. Always check in with your reasons for doing things. Is it genuinely out of love, or is it out of fear that if you don't do this your child might not be kind enough, or won't be "successful," or will reflect badly on you? There can be competition in the kindness department as well, so never compare how kind one person is as opposed to any other—we don't want to create a ladder of kindness! Rather, the idea of being part of the circle of humanity, on planet Earth together, may inspire children to want to be part of the solution to climate change, overpopulation, ocean pollution, extinction of species, food security, homelessness, or many other pressing issues on the global level. We tend to underestimate the ability of children to tackle difficult issues with creative solutions.

A Few Strategies:

1. Understand your child's capacity for kindness and help him to discover his personal power.

In many countries around the world there is a movement in elementary schools called Design for Change. This movement challenges children to imagine, dream, do, and share their innovative ideas for positive changes in the world. Kiran Bir Sethi founded this program in India where she established the innovative Riverside School in 2002. Her faith in the power of children to design a better world spread throughout schools in India. Her Design for Change competition is now in more than thirty-three countries worldwide. Children and the adults that work with them have been astonished at the power of children to effect change in their communities. Design for Change programs are competitive in nature, so be aware of that, but they do demonstrate to children their immense potential when allowed to be cooperative and dream big.

Angela Maiers, an excellent educator, gave a Tedx talk in Des Moines (2011) in which she explains the benefits of telling children, "You matter." She demonstrates that with this mind-set, children are capable of proving themselves to be highly motivated, creative, and excellent problem-solvers for the good of their societies. I would add that children matter, not *because* they are capable of great things, but *regardless* of their capability.

In North America, many Jewish children have a ceremony when they turn thirteen. It has become customary for them to undertake a social action project or fund-raising event to demonstrate their emerging adult responsibilities and capabilities in the world. These can be small or large and are designed to help the adolescent realize his or her potential to make a change in the world. Time and again these projects have shown how children are capable of tapping into immense kindness in creative ways.

Don't underestimate your child's potential to be creative, helpful, and inspired to do good in the world, but at the same time don't put pressure on them to be the next Gandhi! Giving age-appropriate household chores is the best way to begin to allow your child to see himself or herself as competent and of help to others. This is the way in which they develop the life skills that will stand them in good stead throughout their lives.

2. Engage in kind acts, fund-raising, or awareness projects as a family.

Do this because you want to, not to make your children kind. Children have a radar for that kind of manipulation. Rather, do it because you know it is the right thing for you to do. Your heart must be in it for the right reasons, and only involve your children if they feel good about it too.

Here's a short list of things that can be done rather easily:

- collect small soaps and shampoos from friends and neighbors to distribute to the homeless,
- bake dog treats and collect used towels to take to a dog shelter,
- hold book swaps or toy swaps to raise money for a worthy cause, and donate leftovers,
- collect teddy bears to give to police or firefighters so that they have toys on hand for children who have been in an accident or witnessed a crime,
- collect cell phones to give to crossing guards or others who may need to dial the emergency number,
- raise awareness of the need for soccer shoes for Third-World countries by selling brightly colored laces to wear in sneakers and using the proceeds to buy soccer shoes to send overseas,
- collect used winter coats and sleeping bags to take to a homeless shelter,

- divide plants that have multiplied, put them in decorated pots, and give them away to elders,
- organize a bingo game at a home for the aged,
- volunteer at a dog or cat shelter,
- gather some friends and head to the beach with garbage bags and plastic gloves to pick up candy wrappers and other trash,
- collect bottles from people who can't get out to take to the recycling depot. Ask if you can contribute the refunds to a charity,
- do random acts of kindness such as feeding a parking meter that has expired or paying for the coffee of the person in line behind you,
- hold a garage sale to raise money or donate goods for flood or fire victims.

There are examples too numerous to mention—you can find many more at http://www.dannysiegel.com/practicalprojects.pdf, or http://www.365give.ca/giving-ideas/, or in several of the books listed in the resources (Appendix A).

In Chapter Three, I mentioned several ways of helping to increase your child's awareness of her Inherent Worth. One of those suggestions was to have a regular gratitude habit. On a Friday after school (or any other day you choose) have your child state the things she is grateful for and then put a quarter into a jar to save up for a giving project. As a family, think about something kind you could do with the money when you have enough. Perhaps you'll save enough to purchase a movie ticket to donate to a gift bank at the holiday season, or a packet of seeds to grow plants to give to seniors at a home for elders, or some wool to knit a hat for a homeless person.

There are some great books with excellent ideas of projects for the planet (such as *Change the World for Ten Bucks*) and resources online such as the David Suzuki Foundation website.

Skills are vehicles for spreading love

Any of the skills that our children have can be used as vehicles for giving love to another (thereby receiving that love themselves). Any skill can be put to use to make the world a better place with a bit of creativity and thought. As mentioned above, we tend to underestimate the power of children to design projects that are both kind and helpful. If this becomes the mind-set of our younger generations, the world will be a wonderful place. All we have to do is know the potential that exists in every child, help them to realize this for themselves without stifling their creativity or doing it for them, and get out of their way!

Here are a few suggestions:

Reading: When a child can read, he can read to a grandparent whose sight has deteriorated, or could practice with another child who has difficulty reading, or could read to a younger sibling. Used books can be donated to a children's hospital, to a doctor's waiting room, Ronald MacDonald House, mini-libraries, or any number of places. Having a book swap at a school is a great way of making a bit of money to support the library while promoting reading among the students.

Writing: Write thank you notes to teachers and coaches, parents and siblings. The art of the handwritten note is rapidly disappearing but may well make a comeback because of the impact on the receiver. Making cards is a fun way to further enhance that impact.

Music: Children can put their talents to entertaining shut-ins, or elders. They could offer to teach a child who wouldn't have access to music lessons how to play a musical instrument.

Crafts: Learn how to make balloon animals, or how to be a clown or juggle to entertain the young or the elderly. Consider using the gratitude money jar to spend on balloons to take to a children's ward at a hospital (older people love balloons as well)—just ask first as some hospitals don't allow latex balloons in case of allergies.

Knitting: Teach a child to knit and they'll be able to knit squares to make blankets for an aging relative or for a hospice, or scarves for the homeless in winter.

Sewing: Sewing skills could be put to making quilts for babies or tablecloths for homeless shelters to make them seem less institutional.

Sports: Children can coach other children, organize games for children in homeless shelters, provide equipment to those who can't afford it, or stage a match or performance that raises money to donate to any cause.

Cooking: Make soup for an elderly relative or neighbor who is sick. Deliver the soup in a basket with some flowers and a "get well" card or note.

Baking: Bake cookies or a cake to sell to raise money for a charity of choice, or bring the cookies to a coach, teacher, fire hall, or any place where there are people to thank for the work that they do.

It can be helpful to consider skills as "giving skills" so that the potential for use in positive ways becomes front of mind for our children rather than seeing skills simply as tools for themselves or to use to get ahead.

3. Appreciate kindness

We convey our values to our children based on what we talk about at home. Are we complaining about all the things that upset us during the day, or are we talking about the kind acts we noticed and our wonder at the world? If we focus our attention on the kindness of others, the news stories about kind acts or bravery, then we give our children the message that kindness is something we value. They will get the message.

Notice who is kind and tell your children about them. It was through Facebook that I learned about a boy named Campbell Remess, who learned to sew so that he could give teddies and other stuffed toys to children in hospitals who have long-term illnesses. This remarkable Tasmanian boy from a big family is an example of what is possible. Not only does he make all the toys, but he distributes them himself and befriends some of the children he gives the toys to. He prefers to spend time at his sewing machine to being in front of the TV watching movies with his family. His motive for doing this is to turn frowns into smiles and spread happiness to children who are in pain. Now that his project has gained worldwide attention, he heads up his organization "Project 365," which you can learn about online. In Campbell's own words, "Being kind and not mean will change the world a lot."

4. Read books about kindness (with caution!)

Read books that feature kind acts but be aware that some books come with a side order of guilt! Always read a book first with that in mind, so that you are not passing on guilt unintentionally. I have listed at the back of this book (Appendix A) some children's picture books that are wonderful to read as they are, and a few that can be read to start a discussion about guilt, self-esteem *versus* Inherent Worth, and other issues.

Books that help older children to be socially aware include the *Harry Potter* books, and books by Elizabeth Stewart such as *Blue Gold* (about the impact of cell phone production and use on three teenage girls in different parts of the world) and *The Lynching of Louie Sam* (a historical novel based in the Pacific Northwest, that raises ethical and moral questions to the reader). Reading books with your child will allow you to open discussions about Inherent Worth, negative beliefs, purpose, kindness, and many other issues. It is also a great way to connect with your child.

5. Be a kind, caring role model

This, as I have mentioned before, is the best way of teaching and is the lesson that children will learn from watching and hearing you.

KEY TAKEAWAYS

Society has tended to place greater importance on getting good grades than on being kind, but kindness can lead to a happier life, less stress, and academic success.

- ❖ Trust that putting an emphasis on kindness rather than on grades will be good for grades as well!

Children have immense power to act in kind ways.

- ❖ Notice all the times your child is kind.

Kindness can be learned by being in contact with kind people—the best role models are kind parents.

- ❖ Tell your children about the kind people you admire.
- ❖ Tell them about kindness you have witnessed during your day.

Kindness is good for our mental health and sense of well-being.

- ❖ If your children notice unkind actions of public figures be sure to discuss with them how it makes them feel and ask them how they would deal with the situation in a kind way.

Your worth is not established by how kind you are, and it is not helpful to rank people in terms of their kindness, but kindness helps us to be in touch with our higher selves and to feel our Inherent Worth.

Chapter Nine

Parenting with love and not with fear

*"There is really only one decision that underlies
all other decisions concerning our children.
Whether we will choose love or fear."*
–Peggy O'Mara

Imagine a world in which leaders work together to solve problems and wouldn't even think of hurling insults at each other.

Imagine a world where the predominant drive is to help each other—not to try to get ahead to get more for ourselves.

Imagine a world in which sports activities are actually fun and athletes are not tempted to take performance-enhancing drugs because playing the game is more important than winning.

Imagine a world in which addictions and depression are nonexistent and in which high gross national happiness is the most sought-after goal of every country.

You might call me Pollyanna, but I can't give up on that vision yet. There is already one country (Bhutan) that measures its gross national happiness—surely more will follow.

I don't think this is as difficult to achieve, nor as farfetched, as you think.

What we are seeing in the U.S. and around the world in the form of unkind, ruthless politicians is the result of years of politics of fear, and fear-mongering, fueled by media outlets that are hungry for advertising dollars. Love is the antidote.

We have to start somewhere so why not with us and with our children?

By reading this book, you have expressed that you want your children to grow up trouble-free, which means happy, mentally healthy, and kind. All we really need to do is raise our children with love and not with fear. That may sound obvious, but it is not as simple as it sounds.

What Does It Mean to be Parenting Out of Love?

In Part Two, I explained that loving unconditionally is harder than we tend to think it is. I also gave some strategies to help to clear the way for unconditionally loving relationships. On a day to day basis for individual parenting decisions, ask yourself, "Does this lead to closeness rather than to separation?" and "Does this help my child to a better understanding of his or her Inherent Worth, and connection with his or her essential nature?" If you can honestly answer "Yes" to these questions, then you are parenting out of love. The key to parenting in this way is to be vigilant with your own thoughts about yourself and to keep processing upsets using the Choose Again Six-Step Process described in Chapter Five.

The best example of love-based parenting from my own life came after I had been using the Six-Step Process for several years while my daughter was in crisis. One situation tested the work that I had done. I received a phone call that no parent wishes to receive. At the time, I was driving north on I-5 from Seattle back to Vancouver with two of my colleagues. We'd been at a conference and had stayed for dinner and I knew I had to get back that night, because my daughter, still a teenager, was home alone. About half an hour before we reached the border my cell phone rang. I had my hands on the wheel so asked my friend to answer for me.

"It's the police," she said, pressing the phone to my ear. I kept my composure and focused on my driving. I had to concentrate because the roads were wet, and it was very dark and difficult to see the lines.

"Your daughter's OK," he said. "There's been a party at your house. And it got out of hand. Some people came with baseball bats and now your windows are smashed. Do you want to speak to your daughter?"

Still driving, staring straight ahead, I said "Yes, go ahead, put her on."

"Hi, Mom." I could tell she was drunk.

"Hi darling, I love you!" I could hear her starting to cry. "Can you ask a friend to find a twenty-four-hour glass repairman? The windows need fixing. I'll be home by the time they come."

The parent I used to be would have screamed and yelled, blaming her for being irresponsible. But I no longer was repeating to myself "I'm a bad parent" or "I'm stupid." None of my old buttons were pushed. And so, the windows were just a neutral problem to be solved. I had taken emotion out of the equation.

It didn't happen overnight, but I had changed. Recovering my awareness of my Inherent Worth had changed my behavior and transformed my life. I went from being a scream machine to being an effective love-based parent, from being chronically depressed to finding joy in every single day. The ripple effects transformed my daughter's life too. This was the moment that she let love in and it was a real turning point in her healing.

So, parenting out of love happens naturally when you maintain your peace by using the Six-Step Process at every opportunity to keep your emotions out of your interactions with your children.

What Does It Mean to be Parenting Out of Fear?

We are parenting from fear when our negative beliefs are dictating our responses to our child's behavior, and to our own needs to establish our worth. To give you an example: if I want my child to be a professional athlete or a virtuoso violinist, I may sign them up for lessons and be disappointed when they do not perform according to my expectations. Having expectations of them will inevitably lead to disappointment somewhere along the line and disappointment is the result of a negative belief about myself.

On an everyday level, this simply means that if I expect them to say "thank you!" to Grandma for giving them an ice cream and instead they just grab it and run outside, I'll be upset and angry because my belief that I'm a bad parent was triggered. That then needs to be processed. Of course, it is appropriate to help a child to understand the advantages of being polite, but this can only be done when the emotion has been taken out of the situation and it is merely a point of information, which could be practiced in a fun way at a later time.

Your own beliefs interact with your child's beliefs in a co-dependant "tango." Your child will provide evidence for your beliefs, and your reactions to your child will provide evidence for your child's beliefs. We lock each other into a cycle which is our comfort zone, but which is not beneficial to either of us! Many of us have a deep-seated belief that we are bad parents—a belief that grew out of a much earlier belief that we are not good enough, or just simply bad. That belief demands repetitive, ongoing evidence and our children are more than willing to provide it.

The irony is that we need our children to be perfect to cover up the belief that we are bad parents, and they need to fail at it to provide the evidence that strengthens the belief instead. Our children believe they are not "good enough" or "bad" and they will gain all the evidence they need for these beliefs when they don't live up to our expectations of their behavior or their achievements in our eyes. It's a perfect set-up, but there is a way out.

We undo this set-up or trap when we process all our upsets and undo our beliefs by reminding ourselves constantly that our Worth is Inherent. This is not something that we do once, but a continual practice of catching our negative thoughts and feelings. We are rewiring our brains with different thought patterns and it takes a while!

When we use the strategies that I gave in Chapter Three to strengthen our children's awareness of their Inherent Worth, we free them from the need to provide evidence for us of our and their own misconstrued beliefs.

It is obvious that some of the things we may do deliberately or inadvertently as parents are coming from fear-based thinking. Here are a few:

Blame

Blame is always coming from fear. Step Two of the Choose Again Six-Step Process (Chapter 5) is the step that does away with blame completely. Any upset or reaction I have to any situation is always about me—not about my child or the incident at hand. Blame deflects the attention from me, which is where deep down I think it belongs. I am likely to blame others if I will look bad by taking responsibility for something. I'd rather deflect the blame than trigger my belief that I am not good enough, bad, guilty, or a victim. In fact, any time I am tempted to blame others, I am playing out my role as a victim. Something went wrong, and it wasn't my fault!

This was a tricky one for me. I have a knee-jerk reaction to blame others because I have a need to look perfect to protect the image I project of myself to cover up my inner monster—the monstrous person I subconsciously believe I am. I would even blame my children rather than have my imperfections exposed! Taking 100 percent responsibility for my actions and reactions has greatly enhanced my experience in life and overall happiness.

Punishment

The word "punishment" tends to evoke a visceral reaction because of its connotations with pain and fear. In days gone by, parents would use the phrase "This is for your own good" before administering a spanking. On some level, they must have thought that it was a loving thing to do! Here's the thing: Punishment is never loving. Punishment hurts a child and leads to separation rather than closeness. It contributes to a fear-based system of behavior. It worsens a child's behavior and contributes to mental health issues in the long term.

A child who appears to be acting out or misbehaving is issuing a cry for love, and an extension of love is the appropriate response to that call. As a school principal, I informed my staff that to be helpful to any child acting out we needed to "Love them more!" In practical terms that meant giving them the necessary attention to find out what was going on behind the scenes and what was driving the presenting behavior. If teachers and principals would all be familiar with the Six-Step Process, they would be able to diagnose the hidden beliefs driving negative behavior and they'd be sure to promote the Inherent Worth of every student as the antidote. It is something to aim for! The same thing goes for parents.

Time-In *Versus* Time-Out

Fortunately, in many countries around the world, spanking is no longer legal. However, children can also be traumatized by "time-outs" because of the isolation it causes. Parenting experts Laura Markham (*Peaceful Parent, Happy Kids*), Rebecca Eanes (*Positive Parenting: An Essential Guide*), and others advocate for "Time-Ins," and that is a great idea. Spending time with a child who is out of control will be far more productive than isolating that child and feeding the negative beliefs that drove the behavior in the first place. Rebecca Eanes suggests having a "Time-In kit" with such things in it as paper to tear, a glitter jar to shake to help in calming down, or a feather as a visual cue. Taking a young child onto your knee and giving a hug will help them to understand that "We're on the same team—I can help you!"—rather than "It's me against you."

Shaming a child for behaving a certain way will also make matters worse and will feed stubborn negative beliefs. Relieving children of the shame they pick up throughout their lives, particularly during toilet training and again at puberty, will be very helpful. Talking openly and age-appropriately about feelings, sex, and puberty will help to decrease feelings of shame that children accumulate.

Judgment

All judgment is of ourselves, and it is always coming from a fearful place. We see only perfection when we are operating out of a loving place—when we know who we are. Our children don't enjoy being judged, and neither do we. It simply reinforces negative beliefs. The only use for judgment is to find out what you believe about yourself—your judgments of others point directly to the beliefs that you have buried the deepest. Make sure you look at them and process them—how does it feel when you have that judgment about yourself? Take that back to an early memory and figure out the belief beneath it.

Resentment

Resentment is a nasty emotion that can build up over time. It is the unfortunate result of love which has been given conditionally. Parents believe that they are giving out of love, but if there is any resentment whatsoever, it points to that love as having strings attached. "I'm happy to fund your education, or help you get started on your own, but I need you to show your appreciation." When that appreciation isn't loud enough or sincere enough or given in a particular way, resentment is the result. Process the feeling of resentment to discover where it is coming from. It is not about your child's lack of appreciation, it's about you—a belief that you are not worthy or some such hidden belief in play. You can heal it!

There are several situations in which fear masquerades as love. Here are a few of them:

Worry

I have an elderly friend who lets me know whenever she worries about me because to her the worrying she does shows me that she loves me. The problem is that worrying is not a loving thing to do. It causes distress to the person doing the worrying and serves no other purpose for them, except perhaps to prove to them that they are weak and powerless—victims of the circumstances they are worrying about. It contributes to bad health (and grey hair!). Consider worrying as a prayer for the worst outcome. It focuses emotional energy, time, and attention onto the outcome that is not wanted but does nothing to achieve the preferred outcome.

The other problem with worrying is that it gives a negative message to the person being worried over. If I know that someone is worrying about me, I get the message that the person doesn't think I am capable of taking care of myself in whatever situation I am in, and that I'm not safe. Neither of these things is true! Worrying feeds negative beliefs—providing evidence of their veracity.

Worrying about my daughter when she was in crisis seemed like a very natural thing to do and I certainly made myself sick with worry for years. Learning not to worry was a huge relief and a big first step in healing for us both. I actually find it easy not to worry about anything now by recognizing how damaging and how futile it is.

Sacrifice

Sacrifice is another fear-based idea that comes from believing that something had to be given up to achieve a particular outcome. Parents will often tell their children of the sacrifices they had to make for the welfare of their offspring—such as moving to a bigger town, a better school district, scrimping on the money they had so that shoes could be bought, or any number of possibilities. These gestures can all be done out of love, but when presented as a sacrifice, they are held against the child in the form of resentment. It suggests that the parents would rather not have done these things—they only did them for the sake of the child. If these were gifts that were truly given, the parents would have received the "energy" of the unconditional gift they gave and the idea that they sacrificed wouldn't enter their consciousness.

Expectations

There are a good many parenting experts and psychologists that firmly believe having high expectations of a child is a good thing. It is entirely appropriate to see the *potential* in every child, but having high expectations of them is the result of fearful thinking processes. "If my child doesn't get into university, he'll never be able to support himself. I'll be looking after him for the rest of my life!" "If my child doesn't get a gold medal, my investment won't have been worth it!" "If my child doesn't do well, it'll show me up as being a poor parent, or not as smart as her friend's parents." The kindest thing we can do for our children is to let go of our expectations of them—they are stressed out enough as it is!

Love-Based *versus* Fear-Based Chart

Here's a chart summarizing some factors that are love-based and some that are fear-based so that you can compare the two lists:

LOVE	FEAR
Nonjudgment	Judgment
Hugs	Punishment
Time-In	Time-Out
Smiles	Sacrifice
Acceptance	Worry
Problem-solving	Expectations
Circle of Humanity	Ranking
Innocence	Guilt
Freedom	Blame
Joy	Shame
Unconditional love	Resentment

Is Love-Based Parenting Too Permissive?

The question that is being asked is coming from a fearful place. That fear is of being judged for having spoiled children. Accusing a parent of spoiling their child is a damning judgment of their ability to parent and no parent wishes to hear that from anyone, least of all their own parents. If this is an issue for you, please note the feelings that come up in you when you imagine hearing this accusation, then process them using the Six Steps. This is not about being accused of spoiling your child; rather, it goes back to a belief that you are bad, guilty, or not good enough. It isn't true!!

There is a common misconception among parents that if they parent solely out of love, they will spoil their children. The characteristics of a spoiled child are:

- ❖ Ungrateful
- ❖ Entitled
- ❖ Demanding

Children who are raised to know their Inherent Worth are unlikely to display any of these traits. In fact, gratitude, which is a cornerstone of this loving approach, is the antidote to spoiling.

This loving approach to parenting is definitely not permissive. Permissive parents are parenting out of the fear of losing the love of their children if they don't give in to their every demand. A parent who knows who he or she is will not be a pushover but will be firm and calm in stating their requests. They will also be secure in not reacting angrily to pushback and capable of "holding the space" for their children. Keep asking the question, "Is this the loving thing to do?" and remind yourself that the answer is "yes" when the decision being questioned brings to light a greater awareness of the Inherent Worth of both parent and child.

At this point it will be helpful to retake the test in Appendix B. Are there questions that you would answer differently now as a result of having read this book? Note how far you have come and give yourself a pat on the back.

KEY TAKEAWAYS

We can examine our interactions with our children and partner to discover how much fear there is in our approach to parenting and to life in general.

- ❖ Ask yourself if your parenting decisions are fear-based or love-based and favor love-based decisions as often as possible.
- ❖ Make a conscious decision to move from fear-based to love-based parenting.
- ❖ Use the Six-Step process to move gradually from a fear-based way of thinking to a love-based system by applying it to as many upsets as possible every day.
- ❖ Banish blame.
- ❖ Be nonjudgmental—accept your child as he is.
- ❖ Stop worrying!

Chapter Ten
Your Role as a Parent

"There are three ways to teach a child: the first is by example, the second is by example, and the third is by example."
–Albert Schweitzer

What is your role as a parent to a child?
Here's my suggested list:

1. Provide unconditional love: This is harder than it sounds, but some tools and techniques are described in Chapter Four. This requires that you, as a parent, spend the necessary time and commitment to learn how to love yourself to be able to extend love to your children in a way that it can be felt by them. Children build barriers to receiving love—these are the negative beliefs that they hold. We have barriers to giving love unconditionally—these are the negative beliefs that we hold. We need to remove our own barriers to love and help our children remove theirs. The Choose Again Six-Step Process (Chapter Five) works—apply it to every upset, no matter how small it seems. We help our children by doing everything we can to make sure they know their Inherent Worth, as discussed in Part One.

2. Radiate joy: This one always brings a chuckle to overworked, overstressed parents! If we demonstrate happiness (by clearing our negative beliefs using the Six-Step Process) our children will know that living is a joy. They will want to emulate us. If we come home from work feeling frustrated, depleted, and stressed, our children see that being a grown-up is no fun and that there is nothing to look forward to in becoming an adult—a depressing prospect. We teach best by example, and so by demonstrating that work can be a pleasure, no matter what we do, because it is a vehicle for giving and receiving love, we give our children the certainty that their lives will have meaning in the future regardless of the path they take. One way of doing this is by setting your intention every day to being of service at work as well as at home. You can also choose to find three things to be grateful for during your work day and share them with your family later. This will help to keep you focused on the positives at work all day!

3. Be nonjudgmental: When we are judgmental of others, we create a climate of fear around us and our children will be afraid of being judged negatively. Our judgments of them feed their negative beliefs directly. If and when a child is secure in the knowledge that he has Inherent Worth, any judgment will not be harmful because he will know that it means nothing about him—he'll know that it means whoever is doing the judging had a bad day. Actually, we make judgments all day long—the key is not to *believe* the judgments you make. Rather, when tempted to judge, you can use your judgment of others to find and correct a hidden belief that you hold about yourself. In my experience, our judgments are excellent tools for self-healing. We have tremendous resistance to believing that our judgments of others really are judgments of ourselves. That's because the things that we dislike in others are the things we cannot tolerate in ourselves and so they tend to be the things that we have gone to the greatest lengths to cover up and hide from our own view as well as from others. My greatest healing has come from finding out what judgments I hold about the things I dislike in others. This is one of the best ways of discovering what I refer to as our "inner monster"—the heinous creature that we think we are. That's where the biggest healing can be found—of course we are not monstrous!! Our temptation to judge is always the result of an upset, no matter how small, so always use the Choose Again Six-Step Process to resolve the issue.

4. Take the emotion out of it: Consider everything as a neutral situation—just a fact—even if it seems emotionally charged. A situation is simply a situation and the only emotion in it is whatever you bring to it—your perception of it, which is solidly rooted in an early memory. By using the Choose Again Six-Step Process you can neutralize your emotion (upset) by getting to the root cause of it (a negative belief) and correcting it. So, whether your toddler is lying screaming on the ground next to the cashier at the grocery store, or your teenager diluted your best Scotch with tea to cover up how much of the whiskey has disappeared, first process your upset *before* you interact with your child—that way you won't exacerbate the conflict. With practice, you'll be able to do this in a few seconds—"Ah, that's the trigger that I'm not good enough. I know that's not true. My worth is inherent." Then you'll be able to tackle the situation as the neutral fact it is, and the problem can be solved more easily. This is a game-changer at home and at work. As Haim Ginott (child psychotherapist and parent educator) said, "In all situations, it is my response that decides whether a crisis will be escalated or deescalated and a child humanized or dehumanized."

5. See mistakes as opportunities for growth: Whenever a situation arises that causes an upset, there is an opportunity for healing of negative beliefs to take place. The truth of this statement can make a huge difference in family life. Now, instead of thinking that something has gone wrong, we can roll up our sleeves and welcome the chance to heal a mistaken belief or to teach an important truth. This shift in attitude to mistakes will take a lot of stress and emotion out of family life and will help to teach children that mistakes are fixable by problem-solving rather than by getting angry and blaming. That's a huge improvement on the typical family system, which tends to look for someone to blame. Look for the silver lining even before it becomes apparent, by asking yourself, "What is this for?" The answer is always to heal a belief I have that "I'm not good enough," that "I'm a bad parent," or that "I'm a victim." None of these can possibly be true. It will also help the child to grow in their understanding that they for sure have Inherent Worth as well. If a child misbehaves, it is an opportunity for both parent and child to heal together.

6. Help children identify their feelings: Allow children to feel their feelings and express their emotions. Talk about your own feelings and how you process them. As parents, we can take an accurate guess at what a child may be feeling based on our experiences, and so it is a good idea to reflect back to them, "You seem angry" or "I recognize that feeling of frustration." Don't be tempted to *justify* their feelings—you'll know you are doing that if you use the word "because"! For example, "You might be feeling angry because your friend broke your toy." No—the anger comes from a triggered belief. *You are never upset for the reason you think.* This applies to our kids as well. Having their struggles noticed and their feelings labeled will give them the tools to be able to communicate their feelings when they grow up. This will help them to identify the hidden beliefs that are choosing feelings other than peace and love. When they are old enough you'll be able to help them process their feelings using the Six Steps. Many adults are not in touch with their feelings because they were not allowed to express them as children, so they find this type of healing work difficult until they learn to identify the nuances in their feelings. If this is the case for you, you may find using a feelings chart to be helpful.

7. Be a guilt-buster: You cannot prevent children from taking on guilt but you can help them to regain their innocence when they do. Check in with them if they have had a bad day or if you become aware that they have done something "wrong." Make sure that they know how to fix the problem appropriately and that they are able to shed the guilt they may have adopted. Innocence-maintenance is your job! This is a reversal of traditional parenting roles—it's not your job to punish your children, but it is your job to make sure they are not continually punishing *themselves*. For example, if your son was being hard on himself after getting a "foul" or a red card in a soccer game, you could remind him that nothing about him has changed. This incident didn't alter who he truly is. It said nothing about him that he messed up—just that he temporarily lost his cool. Helping him to examine his feelings—the ones he had immediately before the incident happened and those he experienced afterwards—will clarify what the trigger was and which negative beliefs were in play.

8. Be a love-finder not a fault-finder: This is one of the principles of Attitudinal Healing (Dr. Gerald Jampolsky, *Teach Only Love*). Fault-finding is the fear-based result of projecting our own faults onto someone else, much like being judgmental. Notice the positive things your children do and recognize the negatives as "cries for love." Then give love to them rather than withdrawing love from them, which is our natural inclination until we become aware of it. When a child is misbehaving we may want to send her to her room or express anger towards her, both of which would be withdrawing love and sending our own "cry for love" to her.

What she may actually need instead is a hug. Misbehavior is always a "cry for love." Children who are upset will tend to react badly—their beliefs that they are bad or deserve to be punished might have been triggered and they are acting out to provide evidence for those beliefs. Reassure the child that she is loved and that she has Inherent Worth no matter what has happened. Her behavior will need to change but being aware of the source of the behavior gives you the tools to help her change her behavior by tackling her underlying beliefs and by making sure she knows her Inherent Worth.

9. Provide opportunities for giving: Chores are part of belonging to a family and should not be paid for. Ralph Waldo Emerson said, "The reward for a thing done well is to have done it." Chores give children the message that they are an integral part of the family and that they are needed—we are counting on them to play their part. Children are remarkably capable of kindness and giving when the opportunities are provided. When they hear about people who need help, or children in other countries who don't have fresh water to drink or shoes to wear, they can be very creative in coming up with ways that they can help. Be on the lookout for projects that might strike a chord with your family. If you play musical instruments, give concerts at a home for elders, or sell tickets to a concert and raise money for music lessons for underprivileged children, or give a musical instrument to a child who can't afford one. Some examples are given in Chapter Eight.

10. **See your children as Inherently Worthy beings**, no matter what they happen to be doing! Use as many techniques as possible from the list in Chapter Three to help you. When we look at our children with love we overlook their behavior and other superficial attributes and see directly to the eternal truth of their beings. Looking at them while they are asleep is an easy way to achieve this! Remember how they were as babies and see right past current behaviors. Remember that nothing has gone wrong and as long as you know who you are, you'll be able to see where negative behavior is coming from and fix it at its source.

11. **Redefine success:** Redefine success as inner peace and contentment rather than as academic success, and make sure your children know this. This is the same as stepping away from the ladder and joining the circle (Chapter Two). Let your children find their passions rather than choosing them for them. There is no need to shape your children into model human beings—they are already that. Be careful with your reactions to their schoolwork, athletic events, or dance recitals by focusing on their feelings rather than your own. Are they experiencing joy when they participate in their activities? Be curious.

12. **Be aware of the difference between love-based and fear-based thinking:** Always check in with your feelings to find out where your thoughts are coming from. Love-based thoughts will always be accompanied by feelings of joy and peace, whereas fear-based thoughts (such as worry and sacrifice) will come with feelings other than joy and peace, such

as guilt and fear. With practice this will become automatic and you will be able to switch to love-based thinking and acting more easily. Our children need us to demonstrate this ability for them.

13. Last, but definitely not least: **Have fun with your kids!!**

Child-rearing is such an important task and yet parents have very little if any training. There are as many parenting styles as there are parents. I trust that by focusing on one supremely important idea—that all of us have the same Inherent Worth—and by being aware of the negative beliefs that take our awareness away from this fundamental knowledge, you will be better able to fend off teen troubles and mental health issues in your children. You will be participating in raising a generation of kind, mentally healthy, resilient children—and I thank you for that from the bottom of my heart.

Appendix A
Resources and Recommended Reading

Parenting Books:

Coloroso, Barbara. *The Bully, the Bullied, and the Bystander: From Preschool to High School—How Parents and Teachers Can Help Break the Cycle of Violence* (Toronto: HarperCollins Publishers, 2002).

Coloroso, Barbara. *Kids are Worth It!: Giving Your Child the Gift of Inner Discipline* (New York: William Morrow & Co., 1994).

Kielburger, Craig, Kielbruger, Marc, and Page, Shelley. *The World Needs Your Child: How to Raise Children Who Care and Contribute* (Toronto: Me to We Books, 2009).

Mogel, Wendy. *The Blessing of a Skinned Knee: Using Jewish Teachings to Raise Self-Reliant Children* (New York: Scribner, 2001).

Tsabary, Shefali. *The Awakened Family: A Revolution in Parenting* (New York: Penguin Books, 2016).

Resources for meditating with children:

Breathe like a Bear: 30 Mindful Moments for Kids to Feel Calm and Focused Anytime, Anywhere—Kira Wiley

I Am Peace—Susan Verde, art by Peter H. Reynolds (A wonderful resource to help children with anxiety. It explains mindfulness simply.)

Interior Design—Guided meditations by Cathy Netter Bregman (CD)

Peace—Wendy Anderson Halperin (Ages 4-8. Beautifully illustrated with quotes on peace: "For there to be peace in the world there must be peace in our hearts.")

The Mindful Child: How to Help Your Kid Manage Stress and Become Happier, Kinder, and More Compassionate—Susan Kaiser Greenland

Mindful Parenting: Simple and Powerful Solutions for Raising Creative, Engaged, Happy Kids in Today's Hectic World—Kristen Race

Sitting Still Like a Frog: Mindfulness Exercises for Kids (and Their Parents)—Eline Snel

Yoga with children:

Yoga Pretzels—http://store.barefootbooks.com/yoga-pretzels.html/

Storyland Yoga—Playful Planet (DVD)

Anne Andrew's Workshops for parents:

To find a workshop or arrange for a talk or workshop, go to my website: www.anneandrew.com

Choose Again Information (for learning the Six-Step Process):

Website: www.choose-again.com

Book and Speaker: www.Diederik.org

Circles and workshop information: www.choose-again.com/circles.html

Children's Picture Book Recommendations— With Notes

Picture Books That Support the Concept of Inherent Worth:

I am. Why Two Little Words Mean So Much—Dr. Wayne Dyer with Kristina Tracy, art by Stacy Heller Budnick. This book introduces kids to the idea that God lives inside them and depending on how they finish the sentence "I am," they are closer or farther from that part of themselves that is God (Inherently Worthy).

Unstoppable Me! 10 Ways to Soar Through Life—Dr. Wayne Dyer with Kristina Tracy, art by Stacy Heller Budnick. This book is full of great messages for kids, helping them to understand their life's purpose. It provides strategies for being present, grateful, and kind, as well as suggestions on how to tackle fears and reach goals.

Picture books on Kindness:

A Sick Day for Amos McGee—**Philip C. Stead, art by Eric E. Stead.** Amos is always good to his friends, and when he gets sick, his friends come to visit. Is it love or is it bargaining? I think this one is all love.

Enemy Pie—**Derek Munson, art by Tara Calahan King.** A delightful story about friendship.

Horton Hears a Who!—**Dr. Seuss.** Well it's Dr. Seuss...

Last Stop on Market Street—**Matt De La Peña, art by Christian Robinson.** A grandmother takes her grandson to a soup kitchen to serve. He discovers that there is no shame in poverty and finds the beauty of the people there.

Ordinary Mary's Extraordinary Deed—**Emily Pearson, art by Fumi Kosaka.** Similar story line to *Because Brian Hugged His Mother* (see below). Gratitude and joy are in abundance in this lovely tale.

Room in Your Heart—**Kunzang Choden, art by Pema Tshering.** A folktale about hospitality from Bhutan. "There will always be room in your home, as long as there is room in your heart."

The Three Questions: Based on a Story by Leo Tolstoy—**Jon J. Muth (artist as well).** "Remember then that there is only one important time, and that time is now."

We All Sing with the Same Voice—**J. Philip Miller and Sheppard M. Greene, art by Paul Meisel.** Excellent statement of the equality of everyone. "We all sing with the same voice, and we sing in harmony."

Cautions:

***Because Brian Hugged his Mother*—David L. Rice, art by K. Dyble Thompson.** A story about the far-reaching ripples of kind acts. You may wish to draw attention to the fact that in this story, each person feels good about themselves because of the interactions they have had with others. The goal for our children is to have them feel good about themselves no matter what happens—even when they don't get a positive response to their kindness. Also, Brian's mother tells her children that they bring her so much happiness—when we say that to our children we risk having them assume it is their fault when we are *not* happy. We need to be able to separate our emotions from our children's behavior if we are to have healthy family relationships. Overall though, the message is a great one!

***Each Kindness*—Jacqueline Woodson, art by E.B. Lewis.** This beautifully illustrated book explores the idea that each kindness has a ripple effect and we never know where those ripples will reach. This is a lovely idea, but the book leaves the little girl who is narrating the story riddled with guilt! By all means read this story to your children, but make sure to ask them how they would feel if they were the girl telling the story and what they should do about their guilty feelings. This needs a lot of discussion. Why do you think the little girl behaved the way she did towards Maya? How would this story have been different if all the students knew that they had Inherent Worth?

The Giving Tree—**Shel Silverstein (artist as well).** A rather disturbing book for adults and children alike—the tree gives and gives until there is nothing left to give. The boy just keeps on taking. I used to read this book to children as a way of showing them how much trees give to us, but I find the degree to which the gifts are taken for granted a bad example. It could be used to open a discussion on gratitude, environmental issues, and entitlement.

How Full Is Your Bucket? For Kids—**Tom Rath and Mary Reckmeyer, art by Maurie J. Manning.** This very popular series is used in schools as a way to help students understand the concept of self-esteem. At first glance, this is a very useful tool. However, the problem is that the buckets are filled and emptied according to events that happen externally to each child. The variability of self-esteem is the issue that is problematic. Felix's bucket is filled because he got an A+ on a paper, but what if he hadn't gotten an A+? Reading this with children and letting them know that their bucket is always filled to the brim no matter what (the concept of Inherent Worth) is the message that we need to get across to our children and students. No one can dip into our buckets unless we let them, and we would only let them if we didn't understand that we have IW.

The Invisible Boy—**Trudy Ludwig, art by Patrice Barton.** This is useful in that it illustrates how a negative belief plays out. Brian must have a belief that he is invisible to behave in ways that will prove it. It would be interesting to ask children if they have any advice for the Invisible Boy—teaching him that he has Inherent Worth would be the fix here! There are some tips about how to be a good friend.

Rude Cakes—Rowboat Watkins (artist as well). A very funny, silly, sweet way of teaching children about manners. I don't think many children will be "frightened'" into saying "please"and "thank you" with this book, despite it being a fear-based premise. You may wish to open a discussion about name-calling!

Appendix B

Check in with whether you are parenting predominantly from fear, or from love, by having a go at the quiz below. Details of how to score it are given at the bottom but try not to look at that before answering all the questions. Don't overthink this—you are just getting a general sense of your fear-based or love-based orientation. There are *no* grades ;)

Are you Parenting with Love or with Fear?
Circle your answers:

1. Did you agonize over which was the best high chair for your child?   Yes / No
2. Are you curious to find out who your child is and what they love to do?   Yes / No
3. Did you look for the school or preschool program that will give your child an advantage when he or she grows up?   Yes / No
4. Do you allow your child to fail?   Yes / No

5. Do you have an image of your child in the future—a career path, or a major achievement?   Yes / No
6. Do you stay calm while your child is having a tantrum?   Yes / No
7. Do you get embarrassed when your child misbehaves?   Yes / No
8. Do you allow your child to solve his or her own problems when possible?   Yes / No
9. Do you choose all your child's toys based on how intellectually-stimulating they are?   Yes / No
10. Do you allow your child to express difficult emotions?   Yes / No
11. Do you make sure your child's clothes are coordinated before going out?   Yes / No
12. Do you allow your child unstructured play time every day?   Yes / No
13. Do you worry that your financial status will inhibit your ability to help your child get ahead?   Yes / No
14. Do you trust that your child wants to be good?   Yes / No
15. Do you attempt to shape your child into the person you want him or her to be?   Yes / No
16. Do you accept your child unconditionally and act accordingly?   Yes / No
17. Do you praise your child's art attempts automatically?   Yes / No
18. Do you talk to your child with respect?   Yes / No

Score 1 point for every odd numbered question you answered "Yes" to and 1 point for every even numbered question that you answered "No" to.

1-5 points indicates a loving approach to parenting—let's bring this down to a zero!

6-18 points indicates a predominantly fearful parenting style—this book can help!

Retake this "quiz" whenever you like.

Appendix C

Feelings Chart

It is helpful to use a feelings chart, such as this one, to identify all the feelings in Step Three of the Choose Again Six-Step Process. Check off all the feelings that apply and then decide which is the strongest one (or strongest two or three) before proceeding to Step Four (remembering the earliest time you felt exactly the same way).

Abandoned	Embarrassed	Pressured
Afraid	Empty	Punished
Alone	Exhausted	Put Down
Angry	Fearful	Rage
Anxious	Heartache	Rebellious
Ashamed	Heartbroken	Regret
Betrayed	Heaviness	Rejected
Blame	Helpless	Resentment
Bored	Hopeless	Sadness
Burdened	Horrified	Scared
Cheated	Humiliated	Self-Conscious
Concerned	Hurt	Shame
Confused	Inadequate	Silly
Cornered	Insecure	Suffering
Crazy	Invalidated	Suspicious
Dejected	Lazy	Terror
Depressed	Lethargic	Tortured
Despair	Lonely	Trapped
Devastated	Loss	Uncertain
Disappointed	Lost	Vulnerable
Disgusted	Offended	Wary
Doubt	Outraged	Worn Out
Dread	Persecuted	Worried

Appendix D

Raising Bully-Proof Children

Anne Andrew

What if we really could raise children to be bully-proof—neither bullies nor victims? It must be worth a try.

What if we've got the bully / victim story completely wrong? This blog presents a radically different solution.

In this blog, I'll explain the root causes of bullying and why punishing the bully and commiserating with the victims actually make matters worse. I'll show what both bullies and victims "gain" from their experience, and suggest five strategies for parents and teachers that will help raise children who are less likely to be bullies and unlikely to be picked on as victims.

The root causes of bullying

In early childhood, children develop negative beliefs about themselves that are not true. These subconscious beliefs get started when a child first experiences emotions that are other than joy or love. In order to explain these uneasy feelings, children make up beliefs about themselves that are not true. These beliefs then feed their self-talk and demand evidence of their veracity, thus driving behaviors that substantiate them.

A child who believes he is bad and deserves to be punished will behave in ways that will bring punishment (not necessarily punishment by others, but always of himself in the form of unpleasant thoughts) to confirm his belief that he is bad. A child who believes he is weak will act in ways that will supply evidence—by adopting a slouching stance, averting his eyes, and giving out a "weak" vibe, which bullies easily tune into. When the victim is bullied, his "weak and powerless" belief is confirmed. No one chooses to be a victim, but underlying beliefs make that choice for them.

Bullies need victims in order to be bullies and victims need bullies to be victims! Here's how the bully and victim belief cycles interact:

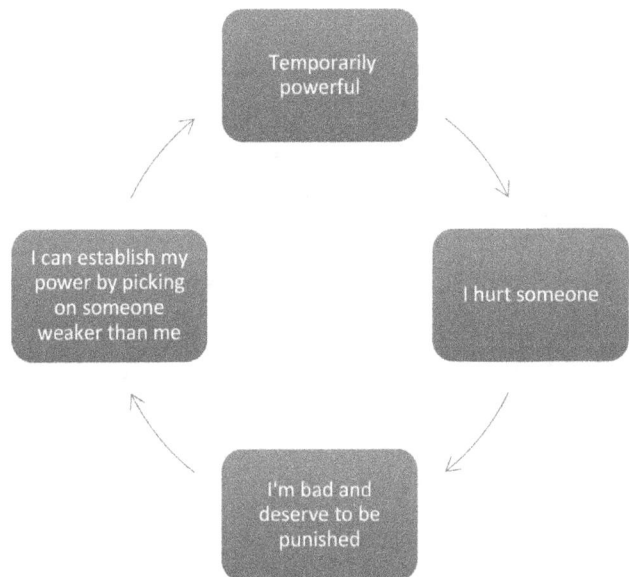

Figure 4. Bully Belief Cycle

Figure 5. Victim Belief Cycle

Ironically, bullies have the same underlying belief as victims—that they are weak and powerless. At an earlier stage, the bully *must* have been victimized for victimizing another to be possible. It is power (a mistaken form of self-worth) that the bully is trying to establish by his behavior.

Anti-bullying programs that focus on the symptoms of bullying rather than the causes cannot work. Unless the underlying negative beliefs are tackled, the behaviors of the victim and the bully will continue. There's actually a payoff for bullies and for victims!

What's in it for the bully?
The reward for bullying behavior for the bully is:

- A feeling of power (temporarily)
- Evidence that he is indeed bad, guilty
- To cover up the underlying belief that he is weak and powerless
- The punishment that he believes he deserves and is seeking
- A feeling of love from the stooges that admire the strength of the bully and want to hang around with him.

What's in it for the victim?
No one consciously chooses to be a victim; however, there is a subconscious payoff. The victim:

- Gets to be right about the underlying belief that he is weak and powerless
- Gets to blame the bully for his shortcomings

- Feels loved when parents or teachers commiserate with him (briefly)
- Gets to tell his victim story and take on a victim identity
- Doesn't have to take responsibility for his experience in life.

Yes, you can be in the wrong place at the wrong time, but you don't have to continue to be a victim once the incident is over. You have a choice to use the bullying incident as evidence that you are in fact weak and powerless, OR you can choose to use the incident as a reminder of the truth of you that can never be hurt and can never be a victim.

The truth is that we are *all* victims until we choose to challenge that idea. We've all made up that we are weak and powerless based on our experiences in childhood. We've been raised in a culture of blame. Someone else or something else is responsible for our experiences and for our misery. So, it is easy to see that all of us have the potential to be both a victim and a bully, and at different times in our lives we are likely to be both. As parents, we must tackle our underlying belief that we are "weak and powerless" if we are to be neither bullies to, nor victims of, our children.

Bullying behavior needs to be recognized for what it is. In very young children we can consider it a cry for love. In older children and adults it is a result of self-loathing—it is driven by negative beliefs. We need to offer compassion to bullies rather than punishment. This does not mean condoning nor rewarding bad behavior. Yes, their behavior must change. They must take responsibility for their actions and commit to transforming their underlying beliefs. They need to understand that everyone has Inherent Worth including themselves and their victims. If they are violent they will need to be kept apart. The underlying negative beliefs need to be dealt with if the *cause* of the behavior is to be addressed. Behavior modification won't work in the long run.

Neither the bully nor the victim is to blame. Neither has any choice in the matter as long as there are limiting beliefs running the show—the beliefs choose their behavior for them.

The solution is for the bully and the victim to heal together. Both need to transform the belief that they are weak and powerless. When the victim and bully see each other as equally mistaken in their beliefs about themselves, and that they have the same beliefs, they will heal and the bullying is unlikely to happen again. The truth of them both is that they have Inherent Worth by virtue of simply *being*. Children who truly understand their Inherent Worth will be neither bullies nor victims. Violence is inevitable, however, if some are valued more than others.

One parent reported to me that her five-year-old daughter, Samantha, was being bullied at school. Her "friend," who is also five, told her she would not play with her unless Samantha gave her the little hard-boiled quails' eggs that she brought to school for lunch. Samantha was giving her friend the eggs every lunchtime. She told her mother about it and they had a chat. Her mother suggested that they share the eggs. Next day, the little girl shared her quails' eggs equally with the bully and the bully did play with her as a result. By problem-solving and having compassion for the bully, the situation was resolved in an amicable way—there were plenty of quails' eggs to go around. Note, however, that this is only a *temporary* solution—the bullying behavior has not been solved and will eventually repeat in some form because the bully has not healed the cause of her bullying, and Samantha didn't tackle the cause of her upset, which had nothing to do with the eggs.

The important points are that:

1. The parent in this story looked at her own "inner lioness" that reared its head when her daughter's problem came to light. She realized that she needed to process that upset to be calm in problem-solving with her daughter. This is *always* your first step when you are upset at a scenario involving your child. She was also careful to avoid commiserating with her daughter in a way that would confirm her daughter as a victim.
2. Samantha's *feelings* about the egg situation need to be addressed. How did it make her feel when her friend said she wouldn't play unless she was given the eggs? If Samantha is reminded who she is, she will be able to play with her friend, or not play with her friend, and make a nonemotional decision about whether to share her eggs with her "friend." If there is no emotional reaction one way or the other, then Samantha is operating from her Inherently Worthy self.
3. Ideally, a teacher or parent would help the little "bully" to find out where her need to take these eggs came from. In fact, the girl was overweight and her mother rations her lunch. It is quite possible that this little girl mistook food for love and felt she didn't have enough.

What were her feelings when she saw that Samantha had something "better" than she had in her lunch box? How did it make her feel when she threatened Samantha by withdrawing "love" to get what she wanted? How did it feel when Samantha gave her the eggs reluctantly? How did it feel when Samantha offered to share the eggs?

4. Having a conversation with both girls together, about their feelings around this incident, will help them to behave differently with each other going forward. They will discover that they both have uncomfortable feelings about the incident, and about themselves. Reminding them both that they are innocent, that nothing has gone wrong, and that they are completely lovable, will heal this incident. Trying to fix the problem using the eggs, which were merely a symbol of a deeper issue for both children, can't work in the long run.

5. Samantha's mother also took a look at why she had put quails' eggs in Samantha's lunch box in the first place. The other children at her school are from a number of different countries, so there was nothing unusual about Samantha's lunch. However, her mother did note that she gives Samantha her favorite foods to please her, which was something she had done for her father years ago—to earn his love. She was then able to process her mistaken belief that she needs to earn love.

This scenario shows that bullying and victim thinking gets started very young, but if it is not ignored, chalked up to experience, or dismissed as child's play, there is an opportunity to heal it for both the bully and the victim. As this example clearly shows, there will usually be a healing opportunity for the *parents* of victims and bullies as well.

How can we raise bully-proof children?

Raising children to be neither bullies nor victims involves helping them express and identify their feelings, so that they can be aware of their emotional state at all times. It is this state that is chosen by the underlying beliefs a child has about themselves. These beliefs need challenging with constant reminders that their worth is not established by their activities, successes, grades, abilities, or talents—it just is.

Here are five strategies for helping children to realize their Inherent Worth—the antidote to all of the negative beliefs that are picked up in early childhood:

1. Parents and teachers need to model reverence for all people regardless of race, status, gender, sexual orientation, religion, or any other label. If we are teaching that every person has Inherent Worth, we have to show that we mean it. Unfortunately, some parents are bullies as are some teachers. Working with your own negative beliefs by using the Choose Again Six-Step Process or any other way to heal beliefs will be necessary before you can effectively help your children.
2. Remind your children that their worth is not established by force nor by any other external means, but is intrinsic and maximal. It doesn't change no matter what happens to them, what they do or don't do. This will need reinforcing as they grow up in as

many different ways as possible. Always challenge the negative things that children say about themselves. Is it true? No, it *never* is.

3. Don't give hidden messages to children. When you worry about a "victim" you inadvertently give them the message that they are not safe, that they are weak and powerless, which confirms their status as a victim. A child who has been bullied will need to be reminded that it said nothing about them that they were picked on—their worth is the same as ever. Obviously, there are some situations in which the victim is at risk physically and there needs to be some intervention. However, the main idea—that the victim has Inherent Worth (and so does the bully)—needs to be put across.

4. Gratitude practice. Instituting a family gratitude practice is possibly the most effective strategy for raising bully-proof kids. Thinking of all the things that we have to be grateful for has been shown to increase happiness and sense of worth. Having and maintaining a sense of wonder at the world goes a long way to helping children be kind and not mean. We feel our Inherent Worth when we are expressing gratitude. Being grateful is antithetical to being mean or needing to take something from someone else.

5. Meditation and mindfulness practices help children to feel their Inherent Worth. These practices, built up over time, help them to focus on the present moment, giving them relief from anxiety, worries, and other feelings that promote "victim" thinking. It also helps them to understand that thoughts are meaningless and can be

controlled—thoughts are not in control of us unless we let them be. There are numerous mindfulness and meditation practices that can be found on line for children of all ages.

Healing negative beliefs that we are "weak and powerless" and adopting the sure knowledge that we are Inherently Worthy along with every other person on this earth will result in a kinder society. We can't afford to ignore this approach at a time when politicians in many parts of the world are modeling bullying behavior and our children are watching.

Appendix E

The Radiance of the Lights

Anne Andrew

The puzzled Ruler stared at the twelve flame-shaped glass bulbs arranged in a row on a mahogany shelf in her book-lined study. Although their golden glow had once filled the whole room with radiant light, now only one shone brightly. The others were so dim they barely cast a shadow.

The Ruler couldn't understand it. The lights had been in her family ever since her grandfather, a wise and much loved teacher, had received them from an elderly rabbi under mysterious circumstances. Each light, she had been told, represented one school district. As long as the students in that district were inspired, the light for that district would burn brightly. But if the children failed to learn what was important to learn, or if the teachers were not wise enough, the light would dim.

How was it possible, thought the Ruler, that eleven of the lights were now dimming? After all, the Ruler valued education so highly that she spent more money to hire the best mathematicians, scientists, philosophers and poets to teach in her schools than she spent on all the rest of her departments combined. Why then were eleven of the districts failing to educate their students? And what was the secret of the one successful district? She had to find out what had gone right there and wrong everywhere else.

The Ruler sighed as she devised her plan. She'd have to consult her Chief of Staff, of course, and for that she would have to brace herself. That man was so prim and proper that he would undoubtedly dress up in an expensive suit and tie, polished shoes, and a starched white shirt. And he would stiffly bow when he entered the room and stand at attention, and, of course, expect the Ruler to behave in the same way, dressed in her best suit, even on a hot day. How the Ruler disliked such formality! How she wished that she could just relax, wear comfortable clothes, eat fries with her fingers, and joke around with a good friend from time to time. Instead, her position as Ruler kept her remote and rather lonely. But what choice did she have? She needed her Chief of Staff, so, after putting on her formal attire, the Ruler sent for him.

The Chief of Staff came at a run to serve his Ruler, asking what he could do for her. The Ruler explained about her grandfather's lights, explaining that she was worried about the declining state of education in much of the country. They must discover why students were not learning what was most important to learn, and discover the secret of the one bright spot in the district furthest from the Ruler's Residence. She told the Chief of Staff about her plan.

"You must travel to one of the districts where the lights have dimmed. Find a student there and ask him how he spends his time. Then go to the furthermost district, where the light shines brightly. Find a student there and ask her how she spends her time."

The Chief of Staff bowed deeply (as expected), thanked the Ruler for giving him such an important mission, and left to carry it out. He traveled north to the first town outside the capital city. There he came across several students kicking a ball around during recess. He called one of them over and asked him his name.

"I'm Jonathan," he replied. "Who are you?"

"I work at the Ruler's Residence. I'm the Chief of Staff. The Ruler would like to know how you spend your time, Jonathan. Please tell me."

"Well," replied Jonathan, "I work very hard at school all day because I want to be a doctor. Then I spend time visiting the Home for the Aged, and in the evening I practice my clarinet."

Thanking Jonathan for sharing his impressive schedule, the Chief of Staff traveled onwards to a town located in the district represented by the brightly burning light. There he found a group of students sitting together in conversation in the schoolyard. He overheard them discussing the Torah verse that their teacher had shared with them that day. They sounded delighted with this new treasure and were eager to share their opinions. One of the girls noticed the Chief of Staff standing nearby and asked if he would like to join them.

"I'm Miriam," she said introducing herself. "Can I help you?"

The Chief of Staff explained that he was from the Ruler's Residence on a mission to find out how the students spent their time. Would she please tell him how she spent her time?

"Well," said Miriam, "I work hard at school all day because I want to be a doctor. I visit the Home for the Aged in the afternoon, and in the evening I practice my clarinet."

The Chief of Staff thanked Miriam for helping him with his task, and set off to make his report to the Ruler.

As soon as the Chief of Staff returned, the Ruler called a meeting to hear about the students. The Chief of Staff was just as puzzled as the Ruler by the similarities in Jonathan's and Miriam's schedules. Their behavior didn't begin to explain the difference in the radiance of the lights. The Ruler scratched her head, rubbed her chin, and eventually called her wisest advisor, her Rabbi.

The Rabbi came as soon as she had finished her afternoon hospital visits. With careful attention, she listened as the Ruler and her Chief of Staff told her about the problem indicated by the lights and of their failed attempt to find out what had gone wrong with the schools in all but one district.

"Ah," said the Rabbi, "you must ask a different question. Go back and find Jonathan and Miriam. Ask them *why* they spend their time as they do. Then you will have a vital clue to the puzzle of the brightness and the dimming of the lights."

The Ruler told the Chief of Staff to go and do as the Rabbi suggested. Bowing low and thanking the Ruler and the Rabbi for giving him such an important mission, he set off again on his journey to find Jonathan and Miriam.

The Chief of Staff found Jonathan shooting hoops with his friends at recess. He called Jonathan over and asked him,

"Why do you study hard in school, visit the Home for the Aged, and play clarinet?"

"My father is a famous surgeon," answered Jonathan, "and I feel pressured to follow in his footsteps. If I can get high enough grades to be accepted into medical school, I'll be able to become a plastic surgeon, attract famous clients, and make a lot of money. Then my parents will be proud of me."

Jonathan continued, "I pay a quick trip after school to the Home for the Aged so that I can get the volunteer hours I need in order to graduate. And I play the clarinet because it looks good on my resume. I need a good-looking resume to get into medical school."

Thanking Jonathan for his honest reply, the Chief of Staff continued on his journey to find Miriam. He found her in the school cafeteria, helping younger students sort leftovers from their lunch into compost and recycling bins. She smiled and waved when she noticed the Chief of Staff approaching.

"Miriam," he asked, "why do you spend your time working hard at school, visiting elders in the Home for the Aged, and playing your clarinet?"

"Well," said Miriam, "I try to do well in school because I want to become a plastic surgeon. I have heard about a country where there is an unusual number of babies born with cleft palates. If I have the right skills, I'll be able to operate and help them live normal lives, free from the social isolation they would otherwise face. I visit the Home for the Aged in order to learn from the woman in charge of the volunteers. She is an expert in the art of Gentle Human Touch, something I want to master.

"I've learned to play the clarinet so that I can entertain the elders at the home, and the children in the hospital, or maybe one day give a concert to raise funds for the cleft palate operations. It's a *mitzvah* skill that I have always wanted to have."

The Chief of Staff decided to take the initiative and ask Miriam a further question.

"Miriam," he began, "who inspired you to want to help others as much as you do?"

"We have a very special Torah teacher in this district," she explained. "He travels from town to town, teaching verses of Torah that inspire us to fix the world, to give *tzedakah* and perform acts of lovingkindness. He finds people who demonstrate unusual kindness to others, helps them to do their work by giving them money or whatever supplies they need, and brings students to meet them so that we can learn to be kind, too."

"Where can I find this fine teacher?" asked the Chief of Staff excitedly.

"It's lunch time, so there's a very good chance he'll be at the Shwarma Café across the street. His name is Danny."

Miriam pointed towards the café, and the Chief of Staff set off to find this splendid Torah-teaching sage.

When he got to the Shwarma Café, the Chief of Staff sat in the corner where he could observe the group of men enjoying their meal at a table in the middle of the room. He asked the waitress if she knew which one was Danny. She explained that he was the one with the beard, wearing the blue Hawaiian shirt. The Chief of Staff's jaw dropped. This man was not like any sage he had ever seen before. He was eating fries with his fingers from his friend's plate, and laughing raucously at a joke that had just been shared. Disappointed, the Chief of Staff finished his lunch quickly, getting indigestion in his haste to leave the café and return to the Ruler to make his report.

Back at the Residence, the Ruler was waiting anxiously to hear from her Chief of Staff and to gain a clue to the mystery of the lights. As soon as the man returned, the meeting was called. The Chief of Staff, stiffly dressed as usual in his formal fineness, the Ruler uncomfortable in her suit, and the Rabbi wearing her best *kippah,* met in the Ruler's study. The Chief of Staff reported on what he had discovered about why Jonathan and Miriam spent their time the way they did.

The Rabbi nodded and smiled, knowing that her question had indeed revealed an important difference in what was inspiring these two students, a clue that explained the difference in the radiance of the lights. The Ruler scratched her head and rubbed her chin, but before she said anything, the Chief of Staff cleared his throat, puffed out his chest and said, "Your Excellency, I took it upon myself to ask a further question of Miriam. I asked her if someone had inspired her to be so kind. She told me of a remarkable Torah teacher who travels from town to town in that district. He teaches verses that emphasize kindness, and which teach about how to give to others and how to fix the world. He finds remarkable people who do good things, supports them in their work, and has them teach students the best ways to be kind, too."

"Well done!" said the Ruler. "I must meet this sage! Bring him to me at once!" she commanded.

The Chief of Staff nervously shifted his weight from one foot to the other, looked at the Ruler, then down at his feet.

"He is not a typical sage, Your Excellency," he began. "You see, he might not wear a suit and tie to meet with you. Perhaps he'll even wear a Hawaiian shirt and shorts. And he might eat food from your plate with his fingers. He may even tell a joke on a solemn occasion! I am not sure that he is fit for the Ruler's Residence."

The Ruler threw back her head, gave a laugh that was so deep it seemed to come from her toes, and demanded that no time be wasted in bringing this wonderful man to the Ruler's Residence. The Chief of Staff was hastily dispatched to find the teacher and to bring him to meet the Ruler. And he did.

Danny arrived at the Ruler's Residence, carrying a shoulder bag with Torah texts and samples from *mitzvah* projects protruding from its ruptured seams. He shook the Ruler's hand, and then, with a few questions, quickly established that he knew five of the Ruler's own teachers from elementary school and also shared the Ruler's love of sushi. After requesting that the Ruler consider one particular verse of Torah for later discussion, Danny spotted a sofa, headed straight for it, put his feet up, and promptly fell asleep.

The Ruler knew immediately that Danny held the answer to the radiance of the lights. And so, the very next day, the Ruler appointed Danny as Secretary of Education for the whole country. And the Ruler also knew that she had finally found the friend she had always wanted. When she was with Danny, she could discuss Torah over French fries, dispense with wearing a formal suit to meetings, and always find an appreciative audience for her jokes.

Over time, all the other lights grew brighter. When other rulers and leaders asked the Ruler how this had been achieved, she proudly pointed to the new curriculum that her Secretary of Education had introduced. In addition to mathematics, science and Torah, the students were now also learning dignity-restoration, dream-weaving, world-fixing, hope-giving, soul-repairing and numerous *mitzvah* skills. Parents were happy that their children were growing up to be *mensches*, even if they did not all become doctors.

Within five years all the lights were back to full strength, and the citizens were happier than ever. Even the Chief of Staff relaxed a little and tried wearing a Hawaiian shirt instead of a suit once in awhile. In celebration of the lights' regaining their radiance, the Ruler held a banquet. Danny sat in the place of honor at the Ruler's right side. Only the Ruler noticed and smiled as Danny reached over to help himself to fries from the Ruler's plate.

First published in "New Mitzvah Stories for the Whole Family," edited by Goldie Milgram and Ellen Frankel (New York: Reclaiming Judaism Press, 2014.)

Appendix F

References and Citations

Introduction

...77 percent of children

BullyingStatistics.org. "School Bullying Statistics." Accessed Oct. 12, 2018. http://www.bullyingstatistics.org/content/school-bullying-statistics.html.

...80 percent of ten-year-old girls

Lawrence, S.D. "80% of 10-year-old Girls Have Dieted," *Education News*, July 5, 2012. https://www.educationnews.org/parenting/80-of-10-year-old-girls-have-dieted/.

...using the Choose Again Six-Step Process

Wolsak, Diederik. *Choose Again: Six Steps to Freedom* (Napa, CA: Fearless Books, 2018).

Chapter One

One Fundamental Concept

Helfrich, Warren PhD, WRH Consulting. "Choose Again Program Evaluation," submitted to Choose Again Society, June 2014. https://www.choose-again.com/uploads/9/1/5/4/91548160/choose_again_prospective_evaluation_final_june2014.pdf.

Wolsak, Diederik. *Choose Again: Six Steps to Freedom.*

Chapter Two

Self-esteem and competition

Fader, Jonathan PhD. "Should We Give Our Kids Participation Trophies?" *Psychology Today*, Nov. 7, 2014. https://www.psychologytoday.com/ca/blog/the-new-you/201806/should-we-give-our-kids-participation-trophies.

"How will I encourage my kids if I don't use praise?"

Coloroso, Barbara. *Kids Are Worth It!: Giving Your Child the Gift of Inner Discipline* (New York: William Morrow & Co., 1994).

Chapter Three

Smile

Gutman, Ron. "TED Talk: The Hidden Power of Smiling," March 2011. https://www.ted.com/talks/ron_gutman_the_hidden_power_of_smiling.

Meditation or Mindfulness

Hoge, Elizabeth A., Chen, Maxine M., Orr, Esther, Metcalf, Christina A., Fischer, Laura E., Pollack, Mark H., DeVivo, Immaculata, and Simon, Naomi M. "Loving-Kindness Meditation practice associated with longer telomeres in women," *Brain, Behavior, and Immunity* 32 (August 2013).

Moynihan, Jan A., Chapman, Benjamin P., Klorman, Rafael, Krasner, Michael S., Duberstein, Paul R., Brown, Kirk Warren, and Talbot, Nancy L. "Mindfulness-Based Stress Reduction for Older Adults: Effects on Executive Function, Frontal Alpha Asymmetry and Immune Function," *Neuropsychobiology* 68(1), June 15, 2013.

MindUP, a project of the Goldie Hawn Foundation and Dalai Lama Foundation Heart-Mind Programs.

Adopt a Gratitude Practice

Emmons, Robert A., and McCullough, Michael E. "Counting Blessings Versus Burdens: An Experimental Investigation of Gratitude and Subjective Well-Being in Daily Life," *Journal of Personality and Social Psychology* 84(2), February 2003, 377-89.

Siegel, Danny. "100 Blessings" in the author's *Healing: Readings and Meditations* (Pittsboro, NC: The Town House Press, 1999).

Look at Your Child with Wonder

Heschel, Abraham Joshua. *God in Search of Man: A Philosophy of Judaism* (Philadelphia: Jewish Publication Society, 1976).

Listen Well

AVG Technologies. "Kids Competing with Mobile Phones for Parents' Attention," June 24, 2015. https://now.avg.com/digital-diaries-kids-competing-with-mobile-phones-for-parents-attention.

Chapter Four

"When a child is most unlovable..."

From an "In Memorandum" for Rachel Aronin Wasserburg at NewCAJE 5 2014, Los Angeles California.

All You Need is Love

McLeod, Saul. "Maslow's Hierarchy of Needs," SimplyPsychology.org, May 2018. https://www.simplypsychology.org/maslow.html

Hallowell, Dr. Edward M. *The Childhood Roots of Adult Happiness: Five Steps to Help Kids Create and Sustain Lifelong Joy* (New York: Ballantine Books, 2002).

Why is Unconditional Love So Rare?

Angelou, Maya. Great-Quotes.com. http://www.great-quotes.com/quote/1712.

So How Do These Beliefs Develop?

...from an egocentric standpoint

Kalyan-Masih, Violet, "Cognitive Egocentricity of the Child Within Piagetian Developmental Theory," Transactions of the Nebraska Academy of Sciences and Affiliated Societies, 1973, 379. http://digitalcommons.unl.edu/tnas/379

Barriers to Love

Dispenza, Dr. Joe. *You Are the Placebo: Making Your Mind Matter* (Carlsbad, CA: Hay House, Inc., 2014).

Know Who Your Children Truly Are

Don't overprogram them they need more time to play. Play is the work of children.

Kang, Dr. Shimi K. *The Dolphin Parent: A Guide to Raising Healthy, Happy and Self-Motivated Kids* (Toronto: Penguin Canada, 2015).

Gray, Peter. *Free to Learn: Why Unleashing the Instinct to Play Will Make Our Children Happier, More Self-Reliant, and Better Students for Life* (New York: Basic Books, 2013).

Chapter Five

Wolsak, Diederik. *Choose Again: Six Steps to Freedom.*

Coloroso, Barbara. *Kids Are Worth It!*

Holding the Space

Plett, Heather. "What it means to 'hold space' for people, plus eight tips on how to do it well," DailyGood.org, March 11, 2015. *http://www.dailygood.org/more.php?n=7550.*

Chapter Six

Quote: "The best predictor..."

Siegel, Dr. Dan. *Secure Attachment Webinar. PBS's This Emotional Life.* (San Francisco: California Institute of Integral Studies audio clips, June 9, 2011). *https://www.drdansiegel.com/resources/audio_clips/.*

"Mommy, I'm bored"

Kang, Dr. Shimi K. *The Dolphin Parent.*

The Perils of Perfectionism

Psychology Today, "Perfectionism." Accessed Oct. 13, 2018. https://www.psychologytoday.com/ca/basics/perfectionism.

Hewitt, Paul L., Newton, James, Flett, Gordon L., and Callander, Lois. "Perfectionism and Suicide Ideation in Adolescent Psychiatric Patients," Journal of Abnormal Child Psychology 25(2), April 1997, 95. https://doi.org/10.1023/A:1025723327188.

What's the message I give you when I assign chores that I don't pay for?

Gilboa, Dr. Deborah. *Get the Behavior You Want...Without Being the Parent You Hate! Dr. G's Guide to Effective Parenting* (New York: Demos Health, 2014).

Chapter Seven

Purpose

Foundation for Inner Peace. *A Course in Miracles: Combined Volume* (Mill Valley, CA: 2007). https://smile.amazon.com/Course-Miracles-Combined-Complete-Third/dp/1883360250/ref=tmm_hrd_swatch_0?_encoding=UTF8&qid=1540572410&sr=1-4A.

Belief Cycle Revisited

Aknin, Lara B., Hamlin, J. Kiley, and Dunn, Elizabeth W. "Giving Leads to Happiness in Young Children," *PLoS One* 7(6), June 14, 2012. https://doi.org/10.1371/journal.pone.0039211.

Dunn, Elizabeth W., and Whillans, Ashley. "Give, if You Know What's Good for You," Op-Ed in *The New York Times*, Dec. 24, 2015.

Kindness versus Grades

Siegel, Danny. "Getting A's and/or Being a Mensch: 2 Polls," DannySiegel.com. Accessed Oct. 14, 2018. *http://www.dannysiegel.com/gettingAs.pdf*.

Chapter Eight

Understand your child's capacity for kindness and help him to discover his personal power.

Maiers, Angela. "You Matter," Tedx Talk, Aug. 5, 2011. https://www.youtube.com/watch?v=7FHdHUzRnms.

Engage in kind acts, fund-raising, or awareness projects as a family

We Are What We Do. *Change the World for Ten Bucks: 50 Ways to Make a Difference* (Gabriola Island, BC, Canada: 2006).

David Suzuki Foundation. "Top 10 things you can do about climate change," July 3, 2018. https://davidsuzuki.org/what-you-can-do/top-10-ways-can-stop-climate-change/.

Read books about kindness

Stewart, Elizabeth. *Blue Gold* (Toronto: Annick Press, 2014).

Stewart, Elizabeth. *The Lynching of Louie Sam* (Toronto: Annick Press, 2012).

Chapter Nine

Time-In versus Time-Out

Markham, Dr. Laura. *Peaceful Parent, Happy Kids: How to Stop Yelling and Start Connecting* (New York: TarcherPerigee, 2012).

Eanes, Rebecca. *Positive Parenting: An Essential Guide* (New York: TacherPerigee, 2016).

Chapter Ten

Be a love-finder not a fault-finder

Jampolsky, Dr. Gerald G. *Teach Only Love: The Twelve Principles of Attitudinal Healing* (New York: Atria Books, 2000). https://www.ahinternational.org/about/about-ahinternational/principles-of-attitudinal-healing.

Acknowledgments

Huge thanks are due to:

Diederik Wolsak for writing the Foreword, reading the manuscript, and answering my incessant questions. More importantly for developing the Choose Again Six-Step Process—it transformed my life and the lives of every member of my family! This book is about the application of the six steps to parenting and Diederik encouraged this initiative at every step. His tremendous support and excellent counseling are the reasons that there is a book in the first place.

All the parents in my first workshop who became my focus group, and all subsequent groups and audiences—you know who you are! Our conversations and interactions have enhanced the content of this book.

My great friends Maureen Leyland, Kathe Izen-Mondlak, Sarah Richman, Jenny Glickman-Rynd, and Julia Shilander, for reading early drafts of the manuscript and offering suggestions and helpful criticisms. I hope to return the favor one day!

Christy Collins for designing the perfect cover and book layout, and Rachel Shuster for her editing expertise. Steve

Harrison, Martha Bullen, Debby Englander, Raia King, Brian Edmondson, Geoffrey Berwind, Judy Cohen, Gail Snyder, and Barb Early for their publishing and marketing know-how.

Barbara Coloroso and Peggy O'Mara for taking the time to read my manuscript—I feel truly honored.

Claire Shannon, Elaine Clark, Angela Clocherty, Rabbi Yechiel Baitelman, Gadi Sprukt, Martin Engi, Christine Reidtmann, Sharon Mishler, Jen Jaffe, Roanna Glickman, Lisa Pozin, Pam Roy, Beth Stewart, Eva Grayzel, Claire Vogelhut, Cathy Bregman, and many others contributed their insightful comments, encouragement, anecdotes, resources, or experiences.

Danny Siegel for his profound wisdom, mentorship, and friendship.

My daughter for allowing me to tell our stories so that others may benefit from our experience.

My fabulous extended family, who not only provide love and inspiration at every end and turn, but who also got involved in the search for a title and book cover.

My son and daughter-in-law for providing me a granddaughter whose innocence reminds me every day of the reason I wrote this book.

My husband and healing partner, Eric, who has shared every step of our, sometimes perilous, parenting journey. His unwavering commitment, extra cups of tea, and morning smoothies melt my heart. His endless help in numerous ways is difficult to fathom.

All the parents, teachers, and others who will take the time to read this book and help to raise a kind, mentally healthy generation.

www.ingramcontent.com/pod-product-compliance
Lightning Source LLC
Chambersburg PA
CBHW072153100526
44589CB00015B/2212